Christian Meditation

doorway to the Spirit

Burton W. Seavey

With Foreword By Dr. Paul Yonggi Cho

Scripture taken from the New American Standard Bible, © 1960, 1962, 1963, 1968, 1971, 1972, 1973, 1975, 1977 by The Lockman Foundation. Used by permission.

Cover illustration by Cathy Feeman, Chicago, IL, U.S.A.

Published in cooperation with IJN Publishing, Buffalo, New York

Printed in the United States of America.

ISBN: 0-942713-00-1

IN DEDICATION

I dedicate this book to three cherished friends:

To Richard Galuska, whose constant encouragement over many early-morning breakfasts gave impetus to the finished work.

To my wife—who loves me anyhow—and who's fine editing has polished this book.

To my very best friend, the Holy Spirit, Who has continually been faithful to unfold the mysteries of the Word of God, and Who has caused me to appreciate Jesus so much more! Without His guidance, this book would have been impossible to write.

CONTENTS

FORWARD

In the fast pace of the Twentieth Century, it is extremely difficult to be still and meditate. Nevertheless, it is a *necessity* which has been *commanded* by God: "Be still and know that I am God." (Psalm 46:10). It is only through quiet times alone with God that one really and truly gets to know Him *personally*. The author of this book has read through the New Testament once each month for the past 18 years—a total of 215 times. Would that every Christian should be so diligent!

Christian Meditation—Doorway to the Spirit is the result of one person's labor of love for the Word of God, one who has meditated faithfully upon its contents. Much can be learned from the Scriptures, as God reveals Himself through the written pages of His Word. Mr. Seavey challenges the readers of his book to "allow the Word of God to speak directly to your heart." Will you accept this challenge? You will be a changed person.

> Dr. Paul Yonggi Cho
> Pastor
> Yoido Full Gospel Church
> Seoul, Korea

1

THE CHALLENGE

Why does anyone spend thousands of arduous hours writing a book...any book? There are perhaps as many replies to that question as there are authors: the prestige of having one's name on the dust cover of a book; or the prospect of financial remuneration. Perhaps it is simply the immortalization that comes with having one's manuscript published; or the subsequent popularity that attaches itself to the author of a well-read book. I assure you that this book was written for none of the above reasons. The only justification I can offer for its creation is that it deals with a topic that *needed* to be written about, and I felt the Holy Spirit impressing me to do so.

Although the background material was gathered over the course of some 15 years, and serious thought of actually writing this book had been hovering in my mind for over two years, the final decision to accept this commission from the Lord was not easily undertaken. There were numerous struggles both from within and without as I wrestled with my own inadequacy to convey the revelations from Scripture which had been planted in my spirit.

This book is not intended to be (but by its very nature it *is*) controversial. The Holy Spirit's motive for inspiring this manuscript was not to stir up a storm of conflict among believers, but to simply *stir* believers! Buried deep within each of us lie untapped resources of power as yet unknown to modern man; powers which, if unleashed by the least among our numbers, would literally shake all of Christendom...*and then the world!*

True, this book is not for everyone. It's not for those who refuse to be changed by the Holy Spirit; neither is it for the ones who are content to sit home idly watching television, unmoved, though revival fires burn brightly in their own churches; nor for those who often say, "I'll be okay—I'm doing my best." Rather it is for you who have longed for and searched after truth which would radically alter your divine perspectives.

Have you ever groaned within, wondering whatever happened to the power of the Apostolic age? Have you also read of those *greater works* which Jesus promised all believers would perform, and secretly wondered when and where the church would see that promise fulfilled? Are you among the number who dare to believe that when God's Word says we are "joint *(equal)* heirs with Christ," it means exactly what it says? Then read on...*this book is for you!*

The Call

Let me share one of the most intimate moments of my life with you in the hope that it will inspire you (as it did me) to proceed in search of truth. I had left the evangelistic field some years ago and in the course of time found myself engaged in a very successful and extremely lucrative counselling practice. There were the attendant luxuries: the tri-level home in the nicest section of our city, a Cadillac in the driveway and, needless to say, a great deal of money. Then suddenly the Spirit of God spoke very clearly, calling me back into the field of evangelism. With some natural reluctance, I agreed to walk away from everything for which I had worked so hard.

I determined then that my ministry would belong to no one (not even myself), but would be the sole property of the Holy Spirit. Accomplishing that goal would prove to be very challenging. All manner of doctrines which I had been taught from childhood demanded my allegiance to denominational creeds. (I can think of no worse reason for believing anything!)

I resolutely made this commitment to God: I would hold up all my beliefs for scrutiny; all my creeds; all the doctrinal statements I had been taught were inviolate; and I would believe *nothing*...except that the Bible was the *WORD OF GOD* and, as such, its truths are *absolute*. At the outset (and through the ensuing months of soul-searching that followed) I found myself holding tenaciously to that one truth. I resolved that I would believe His Word no matter what it did to my preconceived notions! I determined to read the New Testament through over the following month and, if I discovered the existence of a doctrine I had previously believed, then and *only* then would I believe it. I decided that if my doctrines couldn't stand the light of scrutiny in searching through the Book from which they were presumably taken, then they weren't worth believing.

The Light Dawned

In applying this formula some old teachings fell victim to the "sharp, two-edged sword" of the Word of God, because they were the ideas of men; but most of what I had believed before was only reinforced more deeply within my spirit. To my amazement most changes which came about were not accompanied by a diminishing of beliefs already held (although some had to go). Instead I discovered a tremendous unfolding of *new revelation* on neglected truths! So, instead of being diminished, my belief structure was expanded and enhanced.

I began to see the believer in an entirely new light—as *powerful* rather than powerless; as *conqueror* instead of conquered; as *overcomer,* not overcome; as a *winner* and not a loser; as being *on top* in place of being on the bottom; as *the head* and not the tail. As I read and reread the New Testament through every twenty-six days (a practice I've maintained to this day through more than 215 readings), an unparalleled drama continued to unfold before my eyes. Truths which at first glance appeared to be almost blasphemous seemed to leap from the pages. Such a preponderance of Scriptural evidence laid hold of my inner man that I could no longer deny what God's Spirit was trying to tell me. There was a position of power and authority for all believers which greatly exceeded any and all of my greatest expectations in the past. It was true! "Eye hath not seen, nor ear heard, neither have entered into the heart of man, the things which God hath prepared for them that love Him. *But God hath revealed them unto us by His Spirit...,*" (I Cor. 2:9,10a; emphasis mine.) That truth is what this book is all about—God revealing (in the Spirit) to His children today what He has prepared for them that love Him—and how (through *Christian Meditation*) you can listen for and hear His voice.

The Challenge

Let me challenge you. Will you dare to lay aside any preconceived notions you may have regarding the scope of the Christian's position, power and authority in Christ and his ability to listen for the voice of God's Spirit? Will you be simple enough (as I was) to allow the Word of God to speak directly to your heart? If, after carefully and prayerfully reading this book you remain unconvinced; then I ask only one more favor of you—read the New Testament through over the next month and simply believe it in its entirety. That was the challenge God gave to me—could I (indeed *would I*) dare to believe such revolutionary truths? Once having done so, my life would never be the same again. I accepted the challenge! *Will you?*

2

AN EYE FOR AN EYE, AND A TRUTH FOR A TRUTH

The Bible declares there was a time when man knew God in an absolute sense, thus enjoying perfect, unbroken fellowship with his Creator. This was possible because man was created in the image of God and had the capacity to experience intimate communion with God in his spirit.

When sin came upon the scene and the image of God in man was defaced for all time, man's spirit plummeted earthward and he could no longer experience that exquisite awareness of God's presence which he had once known. Man then became "...of the earth, earthy..." (I Cor. 15:47a) He who once had been able to say, "I know God," thereafter could only claim to know *about* God.

God had by no means written man off like a bad debt or filed him away in some musty corner to be forgotten. He had a plan for him...a plan of *redemption!* The errant sons of Adam's race would be bought back by the blood of a spotless Lamb (Jesus), and brought *back* once more into relationship with the Father God. Immediately after the fall of man God began laying the building-blocks of revelation through which we could know Him in His fullness once more. You will find that, in every book from Genesis to Revelation, there is a continual unveiling of God's nature and attributes manifested so that mankind could rediscover Him.

Revelation Stops *Here!*

To really *know* God has never been an easy assignment in any age; persecutions have always plagued those who have had a determination to experience a personal relationship with Him. This has been true from the time of Adam until the present and will yet be true in succeeding generations.

After Adam and Eve were driven from the Garden of Eden, they were faced with the problem of survival in a difficult new world where they existed by "the sweat of their brows." The burden and heat of the day were wearisome but God was there to guide the prodigals back to Himself. The first of many glimpses into the redemptive nature of the Father God was revealed when He wrapped them in the skin of a newly-slain animal, an early revelation of the only acceptable sacrifice for sin—blood.

Abel, a man with a tender heart toward spiritual things, fully recognized the veiled meaning behind God's act of providing a blood sacrifice in order to clothe his parents' nakedness. Thus, when he came to present his offering before the Lord it was "...of the firstlings of his flock..." (Gen. 4:4) a *blood* sacrifice. His brother Cain, however, "...brought an offering to the Lord of the fruit of the ground..."(Gen. 4:3), which was not acceptable to God. In a sense these were some of the first "religious" acts performed by man; one was an act of the flesh while the other sprang from revelation knowledge. Cain possessed certain truth: God *did* require a sacrifice. Abel had further truth: God required a sacrifice of *blood*.

The First Religious Spirit

When Cain realized his offering was unacceptable to God he rose up in a jealous rage and murdered his brother. This *religious spirit* has continued throughout the ages, spawning an attitude whose slogan could well be: **"Revelation Stops *Here!*"**

Searching hearts have always discovered new truths (really old truths rediscovered), then have proceeded to erect their denominational barriers, all the while proudly proclaiming, **"Revelation Stops *Here!*"**

Discoverers of "new" truth tend to follow a pattern: first comes the joy of discovery, followed by familiarity and regimentation; then a religious spirit of elitism and pride declares, "We have *all* truth—no one could possibly uncover more than our 'mainstream denomination' has." In the face of that attitude, pity the person who dared to challenge the fortified positions of the "ecclesiasticals," or who ventured beyond the arbitrarily established doctrinal perimeters of his denomination! To do so was to subject oneself to the fear of excommunication, ridicule, harassment and, in many cases, to the pain of torture and death. As history itself bears witness, some of the most horrendous battles ever recorded have been "religious wars," fought in the Name of the Prince of Peace for causes believed to be lofty and noble.

Can you name even one religious group which did not persecute its successors? I can't! You see, the religious spirit *always* assumes command with the attitude, "Who could *possibly* have any more truth than *we* do?" Strangely enough the very ones who make that statement were themselves swift to proudly and loudly proclaim *their* newly-discovered tenet of faith perhaps a generation before...for which *they* were initially misunderstood and persecuted. How soon we forget!

The religious leaders of Jesus' day believed they possessed all the revelation of God that man would ever have, yet along came a young upstart rabbi who upset their ecclesiastical "apple cart." The major accusation made against Jesus at His mockery of a trial was that He was a blasphemer, "...because He made Himself the Son of God." (Jn. 19:7) He not only claimed to know *about* God but that He *knew* God intimately as His Father—and for this He was crucified.

That Jesus knew how much evil the religious spirit was capable of causing men to do is evident in His scathing rebuke of the religious leaders of His day:

> Woe to you! For you build the tombs of the prophets, and it was your fathers who killed them. Consequently, you are witnesses and approve the deeds of your fathers; because *it was they who killed them, and you build their tombs.* (Luke 11:47,48; emphasis mine.)

"Like father, like son." They had sprung from the same mold as their fathers, so it was only natural for them to persecute anyone who would dare to challenge the Jewish repository of "all truth." The very prophets who had been reviled and murdered by the Jews of the past had subsequently been reverently entombed in gleaming sepulchres by the murderers' own great-great-grandchildren. The Pharisees remarked that had they lived in the days of their forefathers they would not have put the prophets to death; yet there was no place found in their cold, stony, indifferent hearts to hear the voices of the two greatest prophets, John and Jesus! Both prophets met untimely deaths at the hands of their own people because of the religious spirit that declared, **"Revelation Stops Here!"**

Persecution of heretics has always been a part of the Christian(?) church from its earliest days and has been enthusiastically endorsed against any encroachment of new truth upon the old. When Martin Luther received the divine revelation, "The just shall live *by faith*" (Rom. 1:17b; emphasis mine.) the Reformation began as people realized they were delivered from religious enslavement to forms, rituals and indulgences—and were free to live their lives *by faith!* There was nothing new about this truth. "The just shall live by faith" had been a foundational doctrine of the Apostle Paul and was as old as the Epistle to Rome. Over the centuries this truth became misplaced and forgotten, only to be revived through the prophetic ministry of Martin Luther. As might be expected, the ecclesiastical fathers unleashed the full fury of the Roman Catholic church upon all who believed such heresy. "After all," the religious spirit declared, **"Revelation Stops *Here!*"**

More Than Salvation?

Out of the Reformation, which spread like wildfire throughout Europe, came newer and more far-reaching revelations from the Word of God concerning His nature and His relationship with man. "Faith is not enough!" That was the cry of John and Charles Wesley as the Holy Spirit's light *re*revealed the doctrine of "...*holiness,* without which no man shall see God." (Heb. 12:14b; emphasis mine.) Again, this was not new doctrine—simply a new revelation of an age-old truth from the Word of God. These prophets championed the message throughout every village and hamlet as well as the largest cities of England, Scotland and Ireland and soon were branded the "Holy Club, Bible Moths and Methodists." Cruel treatment was heaped upon all who dared believe this strange new doctrinal "heresy."

It should come as no surprise that much of this disfavor and open hostility came from (of all people) the Lutherans! It was inconceivable to them that there could be any further unfolding of God's revelation than that which they had. Certainly such a powerful leader as Luther couldn't possibly have missed so great a doctrinal revelation as holiness—could he? The Lutherans forgot how they had been the persecuted and how they had suffered at the hands of the "ecclesiasticals." They in turn became the "ecclesiastical" persecutors of the new truth. The religious spirit had *again* declared, **"Revelation Stops *Here!"***

You're All Wet!

The present-day church is deeply indebted to the teachings of Roger Williams and the Baptists for the Holy Spirit's revelation concerning water baptism by immersion. This doctrine was opposed by all the "ecclesiasticals" of that era, since infant baptism had become the only acceptable mode at that time. Controversy was the order of the day between the "ecclesiasticals," the Massachusetts Bay Court and Roger Williams which culminated in the banishment of God's prophet from the Colony.

Nearly every generation thereafter experienced a spiritual awakening wherein God showed His prophets some old yet *new* revelations. With these truths burning in their hearts they forged onward though the very forces of hell were unleashed against them by the "established" churches. Yet, each new group had allowed their revelation to degenerate into dogma and musty doctrine with nothing left of its initial life which heralded revival in their generation. Subsequently, when the **"Revelation Stops *Here!*"** spirit caused revealed truth to become regimented and stale, numerous "reform" movements arose, seeking to recapture the freshness of spiritual renewal and revelation.

From Dying Embers—A World-Wide Blaze!

The dawning of the twentieth century saw the emergence of an age of science and learning with strong emphasis placed upon intellectual pursuit; anything that could not be measured in a test tube or analyzed in the laboratory was dismissed as insignificant and worthless.

This attitude was felt in the churches also. The "shouting" of the Methodists was a thing of the past. Spontaneous praise, which had been so much a part of Baptist meetings was only a memory they were struggling to forget. By this time large numbers of Lutherans had defected from "...the just shall live by faith" message and had regressed into empty and meaningless forms. People worshiped the god of *knowledge* while sacrificing their spiritual heritage at the cold altar of *intellect*. Those truths, for which their forefathers had paid such a heavy toll, were often laid to rest with their bones, in the cemeteries surrounding many of their churches.

The age was ripe for a sweeping move of the Holy Spirit. But when He came it would not be to vaulted cathedrals with imposing stained glass windows and impressive pipe organs, nor to the "ecclesiasticals" who headed these august institutions. His Advent would be to a few humble but devout seekers gathered in an unpretentious location in Los Angeles, California. There, in 1906 in the Azusa Street Mission (a converted stable), a handful of believers gathered with the express purpose of spiritual renewal. The fires of revival which had burned as beacons in years gone by had dwindled until only sparks could be found. On those few smoldering embers God poured out the oil of the Holy Spirit and from their nearly extinguished sparks He ignited a sheet of flame that was to spread around the world more rapidly than any prairie fire fanned by heavy winds!

Word spread rapidly concerning inexplicable happenings among this "new breed" of believers. Those who visited the little mission came away with incredible tales of people who spoke in strange tongues they had never learned; while others told of witnessing miraculous healings of incurable ailments. Stranger still were the accounts of spiritual ecstasies—trances during which some related having been "caught up" in the Spirit where they experienced visions of heaven, Jesus or future events. The nine gifts of the Holy Spirit as recorded by the Apostle Paul in I Corinthians, chapters 12 and 14 were claimed to have reappeared as a sign to this age that Jesus was soon to return for His Church.

The little band of people at Azusa Street had grown weary of institutionalized religion laden with forms and rituals which led down dead-end streets. They had been instructed by the "ecclesiasticals" that much of the New Testament was no longer valid; miracles, signs and wonders, they had been told, were only for the "Apostolic Age" and should not be expected in their generation. Thus, this new movement swung heavily to the "right" when adopting a doctrinal position. They affirmed that the *Bible,* God's holy and unchangeable Word would serve as their only guidepost. Anything that could not be substantiated in Scripture was to be discarded, while everything within Sacred Writ was to be tenaciously adhered to! This position taken—there was no turning back.

Whatever affection they might have enjoyed before leaving the "mainstream denominations" quickly vanished, and was rapidly replaced by outward hostilities. Antagonism became the weapon of the various "mainstream denominations,"and names such as "Holy Rollers, Holy Pump-Jumpers and Pentecostals"(to list just a few printable ones) were tacked on to anyone who became a part of their movement. Countless services were disturbed or broken up by hecklers; church windows were broken and occasionally the origin of suspicious fires which destroyed "holy roller" churches went largely uninvestigated and nearly always unaccounted for. The devout were often waylaid and beaten while preachers were prize targets for local bullies.

Those who had been baptized in the Holy Spirit and spoken in tongues who sought to remain within their own churches soon found themselves ostracized. Old friends looked the other way or crossed to the other side of the street to avoid exchanging some kind word of greeting. They were nearly always dropped from church membership (excommunicated) if they were unwilling to change their views and disavow New Testament miracles were for their day. As late as 1955 my own and my family's memberships in a Fundamentalist Baptist church were revoked and many Charismatics report that this is the case with them even today. The renowned theologian, Karl Barth gave this definition of a Fundamentalist: "One who knows a bit of Scripture and thinks he has arrived. If you don't agree with him you're lost. If you go ahead of him, you've gone astray!" Barth went on to say, "I never expect to 'arrive' because Jesus is the Way...and there is no terminal!"

Who were the ones conducting these persecutions—outsiders, sinners and the non-religious? Yes, to some extent they were, but for the most part the worst persecutions came from "church people"—brothers and sisters in Christ. Lutherans, Methodists, Baptists, Presbyterians, Church of Christ, Quakers, Brethren and people from every other denomination! The very ones who had suffered persecution for their faith (which had been established on some *new* revelation), had now become the persecutors. Persecuted by those who had gone before, *they* now persecuted those who followed after. Thus it has always been—*and always will be,* to the everlasting shame of those who do not remain sensitive to the Spirit's flow!

Proponents of this new revelation were labeled "heretics" while those who refused to have anything to do with it or them were titled "defenders of the faith." The obvious attitude and the religious spirit which pervaded (and perverted) these denominations was and still is, **"Revelation Stops *Here!* No one may dare claim any further light on the Scripture than *we* have. No one may step outside the perimeters that we have drawn."** These have been and still are the attitudes of "ecclesiastical hierarchies" in days gone by and up to the present age.

It is evident that each group, having received further revelation from the Word of God than their predecessors, has suffered greatly to maintain that truth. They in turn have committed the very same hostile acts of aggression toward the recipients of the *next* new revelation.

Space fails me to comprehensively trace the unfolding history of the church with its unending persecutions in each age: of inquisitions; of papal armies that marched against the Albigenses, slaying 30,000 in a single massacre; of John Wycliffe whose bones were exhumed from his grave and burned by dissenters, angry with him for having translated the Bible into the common language; of John Huss who was burned at the stake for preaching church reform; of Jerome of Prague, burned at the stake for being a heretic (a term fitting anyone who disagreed with the pronouncements of the "ecclesiastical hierarchy"); of John Calvin, martyred; Felix Manz (Mennonite), martyred; William Tyndale, martyred; Thomas Hawkes, martyred...these are but a few! The pages of church history are stained with the blood of martyrs who have laid down their lives for new revelation. Multiple volumes would not be sufficient to record all the heroes of faith who made the supreme sacrifice for what they believed to be the truth and paid the price demanded by the religious spirit which declared, **"Revelation Stops *Here!"***

Let *Us* Not Forget!

We loudly applaud those pioneers of faith who have gone before where no one else had dared to tread; but let us be constantly reminded that it has always been the followers of, and often the leaders themselves who have led the persecutions against proponents of new revelation from God's Word not originating in their mold. Soberly bear in mind that Luther, Calvin and Zwingly *all* adovated the death penalty for heresy.

Underlying the attitude perpetrated by the religious spirit of **"Revelation Stops *Here!*"** is the most damning *heresy* of all. By its very design it is a self-limiting error which, if adhered to, automatically negates any opportunity for the Spirit of God to elevate our spiritual horizons above their current levels. Analyze what the "ecclesiasticals" are really saying when they state, **"Revelation Stops *Here!*"** Affirming their supreme and ultimate knowledge of God's Word, they make the declaration, "There will never again be any *further* truth revealed from the Bible. We are the *last* group to receive new revelation." *Nonsense!* I Peter 1:23b refers to the Bible as "...the *living*...word of God." That is exactly what it is...*ALIVE*...a living book; the truths of which will be unfolding throughout the eons of eternity. No denomination can rightly claim to possess *all* truth—only that they have embraced all the truth that the Spirit of God has revealed up to the present time.

Mankind has harnessed the awesome power of the atom, but he cannot create a world. We have placed men on the moon and our mammoth rockets have ventured billions of miles into the blackness of space passing suns and planets, exploring worlds of which man had previously only dared to dream. The whole world stands breathless in the light of these phenomenal accomplishments...and we haven't even dusted the fringes of infinity. What then motivates us to believe we are in possession of the total revelation of an *infinite* God to mankind?

Will The *Real* Bride Of Jesus Christ Please Stand Up!

If the church, which I view from the perspective of 1988, is all that God planned for it to be—then He owes the world an apology for misrepresentation! If *He* isn't disappointed in what He sees, *I am!* I perceive the weak, anemic, powerless, ecclesiastical church that is represented as being The Bride Of Christ as being more like "The Bride Of Frankenstein," composed (or decomposed) of dead parts with no life of its own. If it is true that "the Spirit gives *life*" (II Cor. 3:6; emphasis mine.), how can a church which refuses to allow the presence of the Holy Spirit and His works claim to be alive? It is time for hungry seekers of truth to arise and be counted; and it is the hour for The Church to lay claim to the greater works that Jesus promised!

Since The Church was born in apostolic power it is inconceivable that the final curtain will fall before we witness a resurgence of the same anointing, since the Bible declares that Jesus will, "...present to Himself *a glorious church,* not having spot, or wrinkle, or any such thing..." (Eph. 5:27a; emphasis mine.) The Church of the last days will be a mighty force to be reckoned with; a power-infused people working miracles in the Name of Jesus Christ, setting the captives free. These will not be cowardly, fearful individuals; hiding behind stained-glass windows; running from every onslaught of Satan and afraid to witness to the power and resurrection of our Lord. Gates of Hell, *BEWARE!* The Kingdom People are coming! A new anointing is on its way which will transform the timid into mighty people of valor; will turn cowards into fearless crusaders for the truth; and will fill the bashful with divine eloquence, causing them to speak as oracles—prophets of the Most High God. This will be the Church's finest hour! We who were born in the *fire* have lived in the *smoke* of smoldering embers long enough. If we have been inglorious in the past, we shall *not* continue to be so with the dawning of this new day. The pages of our history have been marred, but we look by faith to the Holy Spirit as He prepares to begin a new chapter.

I don't believe that The Church, the Bride of Christ, is going out of this world whimpering and whining but *WINNING!* By Divine appointment we are the ones chosen to write the final chapter in the history book of faith. Let us be daring, so that the pages will record triumph instead of defeat; victory rather than submission; power, not weakness. May it be said of *The Church* of this generation that they marched boldly to the gates of hell with banners waving, bent on conquest—*and conquer they did!*

I realize this talk of victory for believers is new to some, since many Christians have been taught that The Church just sort of "holds on," loses more and more ground to the devil and finally, in desperation, has to be yanked out of the world in order for God to save even a "remnant." That sounds to me more like a "rupture" than a *rapture;* like "saving face" rather than *saving grace;* and I find it totally inconceivable that the God who has *never* lost a *battle* is about to lose the *war.*

To be this formidable, vanquishing army we must be able to hear our "marching orders" from the Holy Spirit. When the Philistines heard that David had been anointed as king they came to wage war and were encamped against Israel. The Bible records, "...David enquired of the Lord," fully anticipating that he would "hear" a reply—and he did. God gave him explicit instructions as to how he was to approach the enemy, then directed him:

> And it shall be, *when you hear the sound of marching* in the tops of the balsam trees, *then you shall act promptly,* for then the Lord will have gone out before you to strike the army of the Philistines. Then David did so, just as the Lord had commanded him, and struck down the Philistines... (Read II Sam. 5:22-25; emphasis mine.)

David was divinely directed to *listen* for the sound of God's army (angels) marching over the tops of the Balsam trees. He was then, and not until then, to wage war. In order for him to "hear" what was happening in the spirit realm, it was absolutely imperative that *His spirit* be attuned to the dimension of *God's Spirit!* Be reminded that it was David who reflected often (in the Psalms) that he "meditated" and said he did so "day and night." The sole purpose of this book is to awaken something within you to begin "listening," through *Christian Meditation,* for the voice of God.

Undoubtedly some will say I am in danger of committing heresy by teaching people that it is possible to hear the voice of God through the use of *Christian Meditation.* The gravest heresy of all is to maintain *a closed mind* to the living Word of God and to allow the religious spirit to dictate, **"Revelation Stops** *Here—and so must you!"*

Throughout the annals of church history the priests and ministers of "ecclesiastical institutionalism" have settled comfortably upon their doctrinal foundations, only to be unsettled by some new prophetic voice crying in the wilderness...*"Prepare Ye The Way Of The Lord!"*

3

HANDLING *ACCURATELY* THE WORD OF TRUTH

We need to be constantly reminded of the Apostle Paul's admonition to Timothy, "Be diligent to present yourself approved to God as a workman who does not need to be ashamed, *handling accurately the word of truth.* " (II Tim. 2:15; emphasis mine.) As Christians, one of our primary responsibilities before God is to exercise *extreme* caution when attempting to expound to others what we believe the Word of God says. The reason for this care should be obvious: as we explain what we believe "God" has said, we are in essence *prophesying* and representing ourselves as being oracles (those who speak for God). If we *knowingly* interpret the Word of God to fit our own doctrinal positions, that places us in the category of *false prophets* of whom God spoke in Jeremiah 23:21, 22a, 28b:

> *I* did not send these prophets, but they ran, *I* did not speak to them, but they prophesied. But if they had stood in *My* council, then they would have announced *My* words to My people...*Let him who has My word speak My word in truth...* (Emphasis mine.)

As I have proven elsewhere in this book, the church *always* snuggles down into the doctrinal rut it has created for itself and soon feels comfortable, challenging any and all *new* Scriptural concepts that don't conform to that same rut. These challenges usually employ the terms "heresy, demonic activity, departure from the truth, false prophets, etc." as a form of ecclesiastical "sabre rattling."

Recently a great storm of controversy began brewing within Christianity concerning two books written about what the author implies are "false prophets." He claims the church has been led astray (seduced) by their "heresies" concerning the teaching of "visualization, dreams, visions, inner healing, *Christian Meditation* and hearing the voice of God." He would have us believe that these practices (among others), are *the means* through which Christianity is being seduced by Satan, when in reality the *true* seduction is of a far more *subtle* nature! These books, the author would have us believe, should not be construed as an "attack" upon the characters or ministries of those named in them. Rather, he claims, they serve simply to "enlighten" Christianity. However, I'm decidedly convinced they have created far more *"heat"* than they have *"light"*!

Recently, the two books mentioned above, were called to my attention by some friends who had been attacked in them; *friends whom I have known and respected for many years.* What I read disturbed me greatly since *both* books were *assaults* upon many of the spiritual leaders, not only of this generation but of those gone by, men and women who have spearheaded great moves of the Holy Spirit which have swept *millions* into the kingdom of God.

One of those leaders unfairly (and I believe particularly) singled out for "exposure" for teaching false doctrines was Dr. Robert Schuller, whom the author quotes 3 times in his first book, and *some 27 times* in his second book.

I have never had the priviledge of meeting Dr. Schuller personally, yet his ministry has had a profound effect for good upon my life. Some years ago I went through the darkest, most trying hours of my existence. There I was, a man who had brought hope to countless thousands—*struggling to find it for myself.* (This is one reason why we desperately need each other in the Body of Christ.) Then, a very dear friend who knew my need but was unable to counsel me, gave me a copy of one of Dr. Schuller's books. After reading it, life turned "right-side-up" for me again as certain thought-liberating truths released me from the prison of my own making. I assure you that my story is only *one* among *multiplied thousands,* and it seems strange that a man who has contributed so much good in a very wicked world should have his ministry vilified in books supposedly dedicated to helping the church rediscover basic truth. Is not "love for the brethren" one of Scripture's most basic truths?

To the untrained layman these books seem to reflect a very scholarly, Scriptural approach to the topics covered and have even been endorsed by some well-meaning but *uninformed* ministers who know little, *if anything,* about the occult.

I have neither the time nor the inclination to write the tomes necessary to rebut each point in both books with which *many* Spirit-filled leaders disagree. I will take selected quotes from these books and display the *gross* mishandling of Scripture and the *obvious disregard* for the very "truth" which the author claims to be expounding.

So that there will be no doubt as to why I am doing this, allow me to quote from that author himself:

> It is even more essential, however, that the teaching pouring forth from the powerfully influential mass media—radio, television, magazines and *books*—be *judged* and, if found wanting, be *publicly corrected.* That goes for *this book and this author* as well as all others.[1] (Emphasis mine.)

It is of course the responsibility of each...reader of books *such as this one*—to discern *for himself* what is of God and according to His Word and will, and what is not.[2] (Emphasis mine.)

We must each come to the firm conviction of what we believe and *why* we believe it *on the basis of the Bible itself, not on the basis of someone else's interpretation.*[3] (Emphasis mine.)

In an "open letter" written to an unnamed author (Jamie Buckingham, whom he describes as "America's Foremost Christian Analyzer") and published in a nationally distributed religious magazine, he defended himself thusly:

Did you even skim it, (his book, "Seduction of Christianity," ed.) or just rely upon hearsay? I can't believe you actually read it...you accuse my co-author and me of being "witch hunters"...you accuse me of "tearing down the ministries of some of God's finest men" and "ripping into these men and their books" in order to sell my own book.[4]

I wonder if that author has read in their entirety *every* book of the *many* authors he quotes from so liberally, or did he simply rely heavily on selected quotes provided to him by readers and companies that specialize in such services for writers. Having read (very carefully and deliberately) *every word* of both his books, I write with firsthand knowledge!

James says, "For whoever keeps the whole law and yet stumbles in one point, he has become guilty of all." (Jas. 2:10) The same holds true for the books in question. If an author will *bend* truth to suit his own ideologies in one instance (and in his books there are *many* instances), then the rest of the treatise becomes *likewise suspect.*

When I was just a young boy someone once told me, "You only have to see *one* white cow to know that *all* cows aren't black." You can drive down the highway and see herd after herd of black cows and begin to think that all cows are black; until you see that *one* white cow that changes your perspective. You may have read the two books alluded to in this chapter and thought they were scholarly works and true to Scripture. However, I would like to point out several "white cows" which prove otherwise!

Talk About *Exaggeration...*

The author of those books says:

> The only "slaying in the Spirit" that can be substantiated from Scripture was the death of Ananias and Sapphira. Yet *their sin was not so grievous* by today's standards. They died for their *sin of exaggeration...*[5] (Emphasis mine.)

In a class on Basic Theology we were taught that "A text without a context is a *pretext*;" which simply means that a verse, or a concept, must be considered in the light of the verses surrounding it (the context). To illustrate my point: the author contends that "their sin was *not so grievous* by today's standards." In glaring contrast to that statement is the fact that *God* considered their sin *grievous enough to kill them for it!* Next, we are told that, "They died for their sin of *exaggeration*," whereas a simple reading of the context would have dispelled that notion entirely. *God said* (through the Apostle Peter),

> "Ananias, why has Satan filled your heart to *lie to the Holy Spirit?* You have not *lied* to men, but to God"...then Peter said to her (Sapphira, ed.), "Why is it that you have agreed together *to put the Spirit of the Lord to the test?*" (Emphasis mine. Read Acts 5:1-11 for the entire narrative.)

It is obvious from the text that this wicked couple died for the heinous sin of *lying to the Holy Spirit.* I thought it was clear enough for even a child to understand so I asked my little friend, Amy, a nine- year-old, third-grade girl to read the narrative in Scripture and see if she could tell me why God killed Ananias and Sapphira. She did so, and concluded, "They kept some of the money, *and they lied to the Holy Ghost."* If a nine-year-old girl understood it that clearly, how did that author miss it entirely?

In the Greek, the word for "test" carries with it the concept of "assaying or testing for purity." What Ananias and Sapphira actually did was attempt to see if the Holy Spirit was capable of *catching* them at their deadly game of deception and lying. They obviously believed He couldn't—but they were *dead* wrong!

The foregoing illustration gives you only one insight into how the author circumvented the *obvious* meaning of Scripture in order to bolster his own contentions. This trend by no means ends there.

Contradictions...Contradictions

Let's examine another area of contradiction where the author makes light of people who believe in God's kingdom in the *now:*

> How could the church be expected to establish the kingdom by taking over the world when even God cannot accomplish that *without violating man's freedom of choice?*
>
> (Now consider his very *next* sentence, ed.)
>
> During His thousand-year reign, Christ will visibly rule the world in perfect righteousness from Jerusalem and will *impose peace* upon all nations.[6] (Emphasis mine.)

In one sentence the author takes the stand that God cannot establish His kingdom without *violating* man's freedom of choice, yet states in his very *next* sentence that Christ will *impose peace* upon all nations. The Thorndike Barnhart Dictionary defines the word "impose" thusly:

> *Force* or thrust one's or it's *authority* or *influence* on another or others.

Certainly, for God to impose (force or thrust one's...authority or influence on...others) peace would be the *total antithesis* of his conjecture that, "...even God cannot accomplish that without violating man's will." Yet "in the same breath" he expressed both concepts!

Let's consider another rather obvious contradiction:

> We are not denying the value of professional counsel *for those areas of daily function that are not covered in the Bible* and do not find resolution through our relationship with God in Christ.[7] (Emphasis mine.)

In the same paragraph the author goes on to say:

> God's Word offers the best of counsel *in every area* of human behavior and human relationships. While Proverbs and Ecclesiastes deal primarily with such matters, *example and instruction sufficient to guide us in every situation is found throughout all of Scripture...*[8] (Emphasis mine.)

If Scripture offers sufficient instructions in *every situation* (2nd quote), then where could there be found an "area of daily function...*not covered in the Bible*" (1st quote)?

What Is A Picture Worth?

Our next subject for consideration has to do with a *concept* of Scripture, rather than with a particular verse in question. Nearly all Christians who meditate would agree that visualization plays a large role in the process, since God often (though not always) speaks to us in picture form. For some reason (discussed in a later chapter) we are more receptive to pictures (when the Holy Spirit *first* moves upon us) than we are to words. To illustrate that point, many (including myself) have used the old proverb "A picture is worth a thousand words," so let's see how the author twists even that proverb to fit his own interpretation.

> The old saying "A picture is worth a thousand words" refers to the fact that pictures, far from communicating something precise, are interpreted differently by nearly everyone who views them...The Bible was written not in *pictures*, but in *words* that communicate truth and a depth of understanding that cannot be conveyed by imagery.[9] (Emphasis in the original.)

Let's consider the proverb first, since it isn't even Scripture, but simply used to *illustrate* a truth. Since I read his interpretation (and he was the very first person I know of who construed the proverb that way) I have taken a survey (even though my name isn't "Neilsen"), asking individuals what *they* deduce from it. Not surprisingly, the people surveyed (including Amy, my *nine-year-old friend*) have been absolutely *unanimous* in their opinions: "A picture is worth a thousand words" means that it would take *many* words to describe what can be understood by simply *looking at* and *observing* what the artist has portrayed!

Now let's consider the author's statement, "The Bible was written not in *pictures*, but in *words* that communicate truth and a depth of understanding that cannot be conveyed by imagery." (Italics in the original.) To comprehend how the Bible was written we must first have an understanding of what comprised writing; and secondly, exactly how did God communicate His revelations to man?

Before man ever thought of *writing* as *we* know it he conveyed his history by scrawling *pictures* on the walls of his dwellings and public buildings; he *wrote* in pictures because he *thought* in pictures.

The earliest *writings* of man are *hieroglyphical* in nature; that is, they are *pictures* or *symbols* which *portray* an idea, word, concept or object. The Egyptians who had one of the most sophisticated societies of man's earliest recorded history conveyed their thoughts in hieroglyphics, or *word pictures!*

The far Eastern oriental (Chinese, Japanese, and Korean) nations to this day use a very elaborate form of hieroglyphics, rather than *words* created from an alphabet. They write in complex *symbols* which represent an object, concept or idea, most of which are combinations of symbols, and *all* of which paint *word pictures!*

The Indo-European languages which use alphabets to form words and thus convey thoughts evolved as man's *intellect* gained the ascendancy. (I will deal with the inability of man's intellect to know and experience God's presence in a later chapter.)

Exactly how *did* and how *does* God communicate His revelations to us? The important role of *visions* in this impartation process cannot be overlooked if we are to be honest in our treatment of Scripture. Having studied the Bible one must come away with a sense of *mystery*, as we read of the many visions and dreams (referred to in the Bible as *"visions of the night"*) received by the prophets of old. The words "vision, visions, dreams, dreamed and dreamer" occur exactly *200 times* in the Bible, so there is no small reference to this avenue of God's method of communication with man.

In most Biblical visions, God *first* used heavenly pictures, graphics and hieroglyphics (symbols), after which He imparted the *meanings* of the pictures in *verbal* form. A perfect illustration in point is Peter's vision on the housetop. He saw a great sheet let down from heaven *three* times with all sorts of creatures which Peter, with his Jewish upbringing, considered to be ceremonially *unclean*. God told him *three* times, "Arise Peter, kill and eat...what God has cleansed, no longer consider unholy." (Acts 10:1-23) Meanwhile, *three* (ceremonially unclean) Gentiles were approaching the house to ask Peter to join them in returning to the house of Cornelius (an *unclean* Gentile), who had been divinely directed in a *vision* to send for him. Then God gave Peter *verbal* instructions regarding what he had just seen *pictorially*. If God is only a God of the "verbal" why didn't He simply *speak* the message to Peter in the first place? Could it be that "A picture *is* worth a thousand words"?

Peter's vision is by *no* means unique. Consider Jacob's vision of the ladder that came down from heaven with angels of God ascending and descending upon it (Gen. 28:10-18); or Ezekiel's visions of the "wheel in the middle of the wheel" (which contained all kinds of flashing lights) and of the four strange creatures (Ezekiel chapter 1); or Isaiah's vision of the Almighty's train which filled the temple, the doorposts of which shook as it filled with the smoke of God's glory (Isa. 6:1-13). No discourse on symbolic imagery would be complete without reference to the entire book of Revelation which is totally *visual/symbolic* in nature and remains largely unexplained. Yet all the above visions are merely *representative* of the multitudinous visions recorded in Scripture and of the *manner* in which God transmits His revelations to man!

Why does God employ these rather elaborate machinations to superimpose His message upon our minds? It would seem simpler and far less time-consuming for Him to *speak* to us in *words* rather than entertain us with His heavenly pictures. Recent evidence seems to indicate that there is a part of man which is *primarily* accessible and amenable to God's *visual* aids. After this *visually sensitive* part of man has been reached, *then* God has access to that part of the brain (mind, soul or whatever term you feel comfortable with) that responds to *verbal* stimuli. More about this in a later chapter.

Is Hell *Freedom?*

Now let's examine that author's doctrine concerning hell:

> The final *hell* in which all unrepentant rebels will one day find themselves is *the state of independence from divine standards* that they demanded and the *freedom that they insisted upon to do their "own thing."*[10] (Emphasis mine.)

Since we were offered none, I wonder what scriptural proof-text the author uses to substantiate such a wild claim?

Time and space would fail me in an attempt to write a treatise concerning the doctrine of the literal hell about which Jesus spoke. I would do so only if it were not absolutely evident in Scripture. In lieu of that I will simply refer you to a few Scriptures which speak *very* distinctly to this subject, and allow you to form your own conclusions:

> Matt.5:22,29,30; 10:28; 11:23; 18:9; 23:33; Mk. 9:43-47; Luke 10:15; 12:5; 16:22-31; II Pet. 2:4; Rev. 20:11-15

Faith *In* God...Or...The Faith *Of* God?

That author's views on one of the most well-known and often-quoted verses concerning faith are worthy of a brief review:

Jesus plainly stated that we are to have faith *in* God.[11]

Many sincere Christians have been influenced by *the sorcerer's gospel* to imagine that faith has some power in itself...In contrast, Jesus said, "Have faith *in* God." (Mk. 11:22) Faith must have an object: It is unreserved and absolute trust *in* God.[12] (Italics in the original, bold highlights mine.)

It is clearly evident the author's emphasis concerning Mark 11:22 is that faith must be exercised *in* God. Please understand I am fully convinced that as believers we must exercise faith *in* the *promises* of God. Having thus believed, we then *speak* in faith (as God would) toward rectifying the problem, sickness, or other disturbing or demonic influence. *This* is the emphasis of Mark 11:22.

However, anyone even mildly familiar with the Greek text would understand that in this verse Jesus did not say "Have faith *in* God," rather He spoke a direct command, using the far more powerful phrase, *"Have the faith of* God." In other words, "Have *the God kind of faith,* that speaks to the hindering circumstance, believing that it will be altered, and it will obey you." *THAT* is the truth borne out by the context (the verses surrounding verse 22) and by the actual Greek text itself. Even some of the most conservative Bible translators make reference to this fact in their marginal notes.

Had the author desired to do so, he would not have had to look far or hard to discover that he was wrong in his application of that verse. Yet his ill-translated pronoun "in" forms the very cornerstone for much of his teaching on faith.

It Depends On *Who* Is Doing The *Twisting!*

What amazes me is that this is the same author who castigated leaders of the "Positive Confession" movement by saying:

> How can such *error* be possible when the leaders in this movement *allegedly* put such strong emphasis upon the Word of God? It has been accomplished by *twisting God's Word to make it conform to their beliefs.*[13] (Emphasis mine.)

Need I point out that improper translation and/or the consideration of Scriptures independently of context are also one way of "twisting God's Word"?

Beware...Many Have *Drowned* In The Mainstream!

He goes on to say:

> Most people are not aware that Positive Confession and Rhema teaching, which dominate so much Christian television, far from representing biblical Christianity, *are not accepted by any mainstream denomination. Moreover, this false teaching* has also been *rejected by major Pentecostal denominations (such as the Assemblies of God).*[14] (Emphasis mine.)

The above statement may not be as great an indictment of the leaders of the Positive Confession and Rhema teachings as it is of those who lead those *"mainstream denominations."* It only serves to prove that most denominations are simply keeping time with *past* generations and are miles behind what God is doing in *this* generation!

When Martin Luther began to preach "salvation by faith" he was not declaring a *new* truth; God had simply given him a new *revelation* of the oldest, most classic truth, long neglected by the "mainstream" church. His detractors argued that the "mainstream" church did not accept this *new* doctrine...but it *was no less the truth because it was rejected!*

When the Wesley brothers began to preach "sanctification and holiness" they were not without persecutors, including the *Lutherans,* who stated that the "mainstream" church didn't accept that *new* doctrine either...*but it was no less the truth because it was rejected!*

Those "major Pentecostal denominations" alluded to by that author also had major persecutions from the "mainstream denominations" when *they* began to preach their strange *new* doctrines...*but they had no less of the truth because they were rejected!*

Religious leaders of all generations have had a propensity for rejecting new truth, as is evidenced by the indictment which Stephen cast upon the high priest who was trying him:

> You men who are stiff-necked and uncircumcised in heart and ears are *always* rejecting the Holy Spirit; *you are doing just as your fathers did.* Which one of the prophets did your fathers not persecute? And they killed those who had previously announced the coming of the Righteous One, whose betrayers and murderers you have now become. (Acts 7:51,52; emphasis mine.)

To whom was that scathing rebuke uttered? Stephen was addressing the leaders of the "mainstream" (and *only*) denomination of his day, which would not accept the *new* doctrines of a strange *new* religion: *Christianity! That made Christianity no less the truth because it was rejected!*

Need I remind the reader of the greatest rejection of all ages? John said of Jesus:

> There was the true light which, coming into the world, enlightens every man...He came to His own, and *those who were His own did not receive Him.* (Jn. 1:9,11; emphasis mine.)

May we always remember that it was the leaders of the "mainstream denomination" that crucified Christ...*but that made Him no less THE TRUTH because they rejected Him!*

So, if the fact that the "mainstream denominations" do not accept some tenet of faith becomes our yardstick by which we measure truth...*then we have no truth at all, for all doctrines have at one time or other been summarily dismissed by the "mainstream" denomination(s) of their day.*

Imitation...The Sincerest Form Of Flattery

Allow me to offer another illustration where there has been either *lack of scriptural knowledge* **or** *an apparent disregard* for what the Bible actually says, in order to support that authors' viewpoint.

> Because it is only at this point that a repentant man finally realizes that *he cannot possibly "imitate" Christ...*"[15] (Quotation marks in the original, italics mine.)

It is truly a pity that the Apostle Paul didn't have the opportunity to read these books before he wrote to *repentant men* in the Corinthian church, where he stated, "I exhort you therefore, *be imitators* of me," and again, "Be *imitators* of me, *just as I also am of Christ."* (I Cor. 4:16; 11:1;) Then Paul compounded this "error" by writing these words to *repentant* men of the Ephesian church: "Therefore *be imitators of God,* as beloved children." (Eph. 5:1) The writer of Hebrews (probably Barnabas or Paul) instructs *repentant men* thusly:

Remember those who led you, who spoke the word of God to you; and considering the result of their conduct, *imitate their faith.* Jesus Christ is the same yesterday and today, yes and forever. (Heb. 13:7,8; emphasis in the above Scriptures mine.)

It cannot be argued that the word for "imitate" means *anything* else, since the word in the Greek from which it is derived is *mimetes* (from the word *mimos, "a mimic; to imitate".* And so we may conclude from the above-mentioned Scriptures that God not only wants us to imitate (act like) *Christ,* but also *God the Father* and those who lead us in the faith! Nothing more need to be said about this subject except to ask, *how did that author miss those verses?*

If Humans Birth *Humans*...What Does *God* Birth?

There is a recurrent theme of Scripture which indicates quite clearly that, since we are *born of God* and are *His offspring,* we are in essence *"little gods".* Psalm 82:6,7 says, *"I* said, *'You are gods,* and all of you are *sons of the Most High.'* Nevertheless you will die like men." (Emphasis mine.) (I will not cover this theme in detail here since that will be one of the major themes of my next book concerning "Kingdom Principles.")

That author takes a strong position against said theme, and argues against the use of Psalm 82:6 as a proof-text for it by saying:

In Psalm 82:6 God's judgment was pronounced against the rulers of Israel because they were *acting like gods who were a law unto themselves.* In verses 6 and 7 God stated: "I said, you are gods...nevertheless you will die like men."[16] (Emphasis mine.)

Since the phrase, "and all of you are sons of the Most High" is an *integral* part of that verse, why do you suppose the author omitted it?

As the Scriptures are their own best interpretation, let's turn to them for help in understanding what is *actually* being conveyed to us in those verses.

Before continuing, we must understand something of great importance: Psalm 82:6 was not the *first* time God had made the statement, "You are gods!" This is obvious by the first two words, "I said," which indicate that this phrase had been spoken *prior* to the Psalmist's quote, and was well known among the people; even though we have no other written record of it.

(Another example of quoting a well-known, yet *unrecorded* saying can be found in Acts 20:35b, where Paul said: "...remember the words of the Lord Jesus, that He Himself said, 'It is more blessed to give than to receive.'" Although we have no prior written record in the Gospels of Jesus having said that, it remains that it *was* a saying of His and was commonly known among the people.)

Yet another New Testament quote of a "missing" Scripture was recorded by the Apostle James, when he wrote:

> Or do you think that the *Scripture* speaks to no purpose: "He jealously desires the Spirit which He has made to dwell in us"? (James 4:5 emphasis mine.)

Although James authenticated the above verse as *Scripture,* it cannot be found *anywhere* else in the Bible!

Next, Jesus said, "has it not been written *in your Law,* 'I said, you are gods,'" establishing that He was not *only* quoting from Psalm 82:6, *but from the Law* (Pentateuch, the first five books of the Bible). Someone may wish to stretch his imagination (and that is exactly what it *would* be—imagination), insinuating that the Psalms are somehow included in the Law. To that, allow me to quote Jesus' own statement:

> ...that all things which are written about Me in the Law of Moses and the Prophets *and the Psalms* must be fulfilled. (Luke 24:44b emphasis mine.)

The aformentioned Scripture makes it evidently clear that Jesus placed a *distinct separation* between the *Law* and the *Psalms.*
To prove his contention that the statement *"You are gods"* was not said to righteous men, but to sinners, the author goes on to say:

> Not only did Jesus say to the religious leaders of His day, "Ye are gods," but He also said, "You are of your father the devil." (Jn. 8:44) It was a terrible indictment.[17] (Emphasis mine.)

Jesus never made that statement *about* the religious leaders of His day, He simply *quoted* from the Law! Here is exactly what He said:

> Jesus answered them, "Has it not been written *in your Law,* 'I said, you are gods'? If he called *them* gods, *to whom the word of God came...*" (Jn. 10:34,35a; emphasis mine.)

It is obvious that the first part is no more than a quote *from* the Law, while the second part, "If he called *them* gods, *to whom the word of God came...,*" is **not** in reference to the religious leaders of Jesus' day at all, (since the entire statement was spoken in the *past tense*), but was rather Jesus' commentary on the Old Testament men to whom the passage in Psalms referred.

The author attempts to link Jesus' quote *from the Law,* "you are gods," with His indictment of the Pharisees, "you are of your father the devil," *(which was spoken in an earlier chapter).* Since Jesus never said "you are gods" concerning these religious leaders, their evil ancestry (the devil) cannot be linked to that statement. There is absolutely *no* common bond between Jesus' quote "you are gods" and *these* evil people.

We *must* read the verses in question in the light of how *Jesus* used them. In the tenth chapter of John's Gospel, Jesus alluded to His divine *sonship* by calling God His Father no less than *seven times,* which according to Jewish Law was tantamount to the highest form of *blasphemy.* Verse 18b, 19 reads, "'...this commandment I received from **My Father.**' There arose a division again among the Jews *because of these words.*" We also read "'**I and the Father are one.**' The Jews took up stones again to stone Him." (verses 30.31) The reason the Jews took up stones again to stone Him was: "*...for blasphemy...*because You, being a man, make yourself out to be God." (verse 33). So *this* was what the furor of that episode was all about: **Jesus claimed to be the son of God!** According to Jewish belief, that was tantamount to making oneself out to *be* God! It was on this ground *alone* that Jesus was accused by His detractors, and it was to *this* charge *alone* that He replied when He said:

> Has it not been written *in your Law, "I said, you are gods"*? If he called *them* gods, *to whom the word of God came* (**and the Scripture cannot be broken),** do you say of Him, whom the Father sanctified and sent into the world, "You are blaspheming," *because I said, "I am the Son* of God?" (Jn. 10:34-36); emphasis in preceding Scriptures, mine.)

What Jesus actually said in His defense was, "If God called *human being* **gods,** (to whom the word of God came,) how can you stone *Me* for claiming that I am the *Son* of God?" I believe that is *explicitly* clear when examined *in context!*

Will The Next *Witness* Please Take The Stand

We now come to a concept which is by no means new; in fact it has been bouncing around out there in "theology-land" for a long time—but it *is* interesting. The fact is, it really *needs* to be examined in order to understand how the author *strains* to establish his theological (?) position. He states:

> In a witchcraft network newspaper a practicing witch explains that the breathing exercises being adopted by Christians are "the most important part of relaxing..." In the same issue the essential role of visualization in occult healing rituals is mentioned..."[18] (Emphasis in the original.)

> "Visualization" is the foremost technique recommended by the "spirit entities" that speak through today's most popular mediums. As one who calls himself "Emmanuel" recently said, "The use of visualization is a most powerful tool for you to use."[19] (Emphasis in the original.)

The aforementioned are statements made by people involved in the occult, but the following is a *generalization* made by the author himself:

> ...the techniques of visualization and activating the imagination through looking within *are just as much divination devices as a crystal ball*.[20] (Emphasis mine.)

I would simply ask, "Mr. Author, what do you submit as your *Scriptural proof-text* for that wild *assumption*?"

Now, back to the comments which the author has quoted from a "witchcraft network newspaper" and from "spirit entities" concerning breathing and visualization techniques. If I understand him correctly (and I'm certain I do), his argument against these practices is based upon the "endorsement" of said practices by occultists and demons. That argument is about as weak as a blind man in a dark room looking for a black cat that isn't there! Allow me to explain *why*.

Absolutely *no* doctrinal position may *ever* be established because of endorsements, or lack of them whether by godly men or the demonically oppressed. Actually, if Christians accept his premise that these things are evil and are to be avoided because of their recognition by demonic entities, we are then faced with another, even *greater* quandary:

And...there was in their synagogue a man with *an unclean spirit*; and he cried out, saying, "What do we have to do with You, Jesus of Nazareth?...*I know who You are—the Holy One of God!*" (Mk. 1:23,24)

And whenever (*at all times*, ed.) the *unclean spirits* beheld Him, they would fall down before Him and cry out, saying, *"You are the Son of God!"* (Mk. 3:11)

...Immediately a man from the tombs with an *unclean spirit* met Him...and crying out with a loud voice, he said, "What do I have to do with You, Jesus, *Son of the Most High God*?" (Read Mk. 5: 1-20.)

And there was a man in the synagogue possessed by *the spirit of an unclean demon*, and he cried out with a loud voice, "Ha! What do we have to do with You, Jesus of Nazareth?...*I know who You are—the Holy One of God!*"...and *demons* also were coming out of many, crying out and saying, *"You are the Son of God!"* (Luke 4:33,34,41)

And it happened that as we were going to the place of prayer, a certain slave-girl having a *spirit of divination* met us...following after Paul and us, she kept crying out, saying, *"These men are bond-servants of the Most High God, who are proclaiming to you the way of salvation."* And she continued doing this for many days... (Read Acts 16:16-18. Emphasis in all of the aforementioned Scriptures, mine.)

In Mark 3:11 we are told that the unclean spirits would acknowledge Christ "at *all* times," so we know that similar episodes took place in *every* instance during Jesus' ministry where demons were confronted, even where the Gospels are silent. In every instance quoted above there was a very strong demonic endorsement of either Jesus, Paul, Silas or Luke! If we agree that everything demonically endorsed *is* demonic, we would have to dispense with all of the aforementioned *and* their teachings! This is *especially* true where the servant-girl who had a *spirit of divination* (which the author *strongly* warns us against) gave such a glowing testimonial to Paul, Silas and Luke; *"these men are bond-servants of the Most-High God, who are proclaiming to you the way of salvation."*

Why do you suppose that a spirit of divination from hell spent many days endorsing the genuine ministries of three truly great men of God? If you were a demon and wanted to discourage others from discovering the truth, what would you consider to be your best avenue of approach? I believe the answer to these questions is found in the demoniac's actions. The demonized girl's *seeming* endorsement associated Christianity with all the heathen religions in Philippi and made it appear to be *just another pagan religion.* The demon sought by this means to manipulate well-meaning, but gullible souls into rejecting the truth because it had been "endorsed" by a lie. Why then should we believe that demons would change their method of deception in *our* day, when such devices have served them so very well for millennia?

The fact that some *demon* has seemingly "endorsed" something is hardly evidence that the thing so "endorsed" is demonic. Our *only* criteria for accepting or rejecting doctrine should not be, "What is a *demon's* view on the subject?" but rather, "What does *God's Word* have to say about it?" In my experience, demons have never been known to tell the truth *unless it served their own nefarious purposes!*

Please note this difference also: Jesus, Paul, Silas, Luke and others in the Scriptures *cast the demons out* instead of only *quoting* them in books...but then, *they* believed in miracles!

Trace The *Roots*...Discover The *Source*

That author's views on meditation, as it relates to Christianity, are worthy of a brief reflection:

> Much of the problem results from the gradual acceptance by the church of a *new* meaning for "meditation." In the **Western** world, until very recently, to *meditate* meant to rationally *contemplate* (or ponder or think deeply about something). The influence of **Eastern** mysticism, however, has brought a *new* type of "meditation" to the **West**..."[21] (Italics and quotes in the original; bold highlights mine.)

A statement such as the one quoted above is the result of a misconception concerning Christianity's roots. The author speaks of Christianity as though it originated in the United States of America and is only lately being *impinged* upon by some "foreign" religious rites "from the East." (His argument could be likened to one becoming angry with a Navajo Indian for claiming to be an *American*!) In reality, Christianity has very deep roots which extend far back into Eastern traditions—because it *is* an *Eastern* religion! Nothing the author can do or say can ever change that. Israel, the birthplace of Judeo/Christian revelation, is not a suburb of Brooklyn, New York—it is a "suburb" of Lebanon, Syria, Egypt,

Jordan and a host of other *Eastern* countries. In fact, much of the so-called "Eastern" religions of today are *perverted imitations* of *Eastern* Christianity!

I submit, if Christianity has been changed (and it *has*), it is *we* who have *Westernized* it, and not vice versa!

Seduction, by its very nature, must be *subtle* if it is to be effective. We have witnessed this subtlety in the few illustrations offered to you in this chapter—craftily twisted or omitted Scripture verses which would almost certainly be overlooked by the casual, uninformed reader. These have served as the foundation for *the most subtle seduction of all!*

[1] Dave Hunt, Beyond Seduction, (Harvest House Publishers, 1987), p. 37.
[2] Ibid., p. 50.
[3] Dave Hunt, T.A. Mc Mahon,The Seduction of Christianity, (Harvest House Publishers, 1985), p. 224.
[4] Hunt, The Evangelist, (The Voice of the Jimmy Swaggart Ministries, July, 1987, Vol.19, #7), p. 10.
[5] Hunt, Beyond Seduction, p. 75.
[6] Ibid., p. 250.
[7] Hunt, Mc Mahon, The Seduction of Christianity, p. 209.
[8] Ibid.
[9] Hunt, Beyond Seduction, p. 220.
[10] Ibid., p. 158.
[11] Ibid., p. 228.
[12] Hunt, Mc Mahon, The Seduction of Christianity, p. 26.
[13] Hunt, Beyond Seduction, p. 54.
[14] Ibid., p. 50.
[15] Ibid., p. 15.
[16] Hunt, Mc Mahon, The Seduction of Christianity, p. 86.
[17] Ibid.
[18] Hunt, Beyond Seduction, p. 214.
[19] Ibid., p. 236.
[20] Ibid.
[21] Ibid., pp. 203,204.

4

THE MOST *SUBTLE* SEDUCTION OF ALL

There was a young preacher (or so the story goes) who, as he stood to preach, realized that he had misplaced his sermon notes. He recalled the sage advice of his homiletics professor, "If you can't remember some point of your sermon, quote your Scripture text a few times and your thought may return to you." His text was, *"Behold, I come quickly!"* so he quoted it powerfully as he leaned upon the pulpit for emphasis— but nothing came back to him. "Behold, I come quickly!" he said again, as he once more leaned upon the pulpit for emphasis. Frustrated, he repeated loudly for the third time, *"Behold, I come quickly!"* Only this time he leaned too heavily upon the pulpit, whereupon both he *and* the pulpit tumbled into the first pew, landing him squarely in a lady's lap. "I'm *so* sorry," he apologized, as he picked himself up and dusted himself off. To this the lady replied, "No need for you to apologize—*you warned me three times that you were coming!"*

The preacher's warning was right "up front," and so was that author's. The title of his first book heralded—"**THE** *SEDUCTION* **OF CHRISTIANITY**"; and it proved to be *exactly* that! His second book was entitled *"BEYOND* **SEDUCTION**"; and it *also* lived up to its name! Those books which were supposedly written to *protect* the church from *being* seduced became *the very vehicle* by which that *subtle seduction away from the mystical and miraculous aspects of Christianity was accomplished.*

Jesus' *Solemn* Warning!

> *...Watch out and beware of the leaven of the Pharisees and Sadducees...*How is it that you do not understand that I did not speak to you concerning bread? But beware of the leaven of the Pharisees and Sadducees. Then they understood that He did not say to beware of the leaven of bread, but of the *teachings* of the Pharisees and Sadducees. (Matt. 16:6,11,12; emphasis mine.)

Jesus' warning was given in the strongest of terms, indicating the seriousness of the matter, and should be understood by all Christians. The leaven of the Pharisees and Sadducees to which Jesus alluded is by His own definition, their *teachings!* Let's examine the teachings of these two groups of people and see how the warning of Jesus applies to us.

"...He (Jesus, ed.) began saying to His disciples *first of all,* 'Beware of the leaven of the Pharisees, *which is hypocrisy.* '" (Luke 12:1b; emphasis mine.) The definition of "hypocrisy" is, "to put on *a false front;* or *to pretend to be what one is not."* The American Indians have an expression which defines hypocrisy well: "White man speaks with forked tongue" (meaning, "He *says* one thing, but he *does* another"). By the time you finish reading this chapter it will be abundantly clear how that author has done *exactly that.* Periodically he claims that miracles and healings are for today, but *the most subtle seduction of all* woven throughout his writings, ridicules not only the miraculous, but many of the leaders who have spearheaded the great Holy Spirit revivals in this century!

What then was the "teaching of the Sadducees" that Jesus so sternly warned against? Simply the type of thing we have been discussing—but let's turn to Scripture for the definitive answer: "For the Sadducees say that *there is no resurrection, nor an angel, nor a spirit....* " (Acts 23:8a emphasis mine.) Clearly, they did not believe in the existence or manifestations of the *supernatural realm*—and Jesus' desire was that His followers be insulated from that insidious lack of belief.

Everybody's Marching Wrong *Except....*

Critics have repeatedly voiced the charge that *Seduction's* quotes have been largely "taken out of context." Yet examples are seldom offered.[1]

That *cannot* be said of my brief review of these books where I quote him a total of thirty-one times—*in context!* The most perplexing problem I faced was in determining *which* quotes to select for publication, since there was such a profusion from which to choose. It should be clear to the reader that, since there are so many areas where he has handled the Word of God in an *unscriptural and unscholarly* manner, there has been no *need* (or desire) to take any of his statements out of context! This chapter will serve to emphasize that point to an even greater extent as we discover what is *the most subtle seduction of all!*

The *Seduction* Begins

No one needs a miracle to believe in God....[2] (Emphasis mine.)

The Scriptures are so replete with proof-texts to the contrary I almost feel embarrassed to have to quote from them to disprove that ludicrous statement. I will offer just one here (but will present a *host* of Scriptural proof-texts at the conclusion of this chapter)—"...*many* believed in His name, *beholding His signs* which He was doing." (Jn. 2:23b; emphasis mine.) The word for "signs" in the Greek means *attesting miracle.* "Attest" means, "to give proof or evidence of." This clearly indicates that Jesus presented His listeners with *evidence,* which He must have deemed *necessary* to bring about their belief in Him and His ministry.

> The Bible *does not teach* that the great need today is for a *miracle ministry....*[3] (Emphasis mine.)

What *does* the Bible teach as the great need for today? Simply stated, it is for Christ to be living *His* life *in* and *through the church* which is His body (Eph. 1:15-23); that we might echo the words of Paul, "...it is no longer *I* who live, *but Christ lives in me....*" (Gal. 2:20 emphasis mine.) The fact that we are temples of the Holy Spirit, and that Christ wants to *reproduce* Himself in us, ministering to the world *through* us, is one of the major recurring themes of Scripture!

Hebrews 13:8 informs us that, "Jesus Christ is the same yesterday and today, yes and forever." Who and what He was two thousand years ago, He remains today and will be forever; whatever ministry He displayed in years past, He will manifest today. At least twenty-five percent of Jesus' public ministry was consumed with the performance of *miracles...*because there was a desperate *need* for miracles. Man's physical, mental and emotional needs haven't changed much since then, and *Jesus hasn't changed at all.* If He hasn't changed, then His *current* actions will reflect His earlier ministry of miracles. The great need today is for the ministry of Jesus to be reproduced *in us*—and that remains, inescapably, a *miracle ministry!*

In Search Of The *Holy* Presence

> ...The *holy presence* that accompanied His mighty works was also withdrawn, and miracles became few and far between, *as they are today.*[4] (Emphasis mine.)

Although the author again offers no proof-text to support his *assumption,* let us presume for argument's sake that he is correct, and examine it from *his* viewpoint.

His contention has as its foundation the thought that "miracles and mighty works became few and far between (*as they are today*) because

God's holy presence that accompanied them (Israel, ed.) was *withdrawn.*" If that be true, then the *converse* must *also* be true: **if God's HOLY PRESENCE is with a person or persons, miracles and mighty works** *would be manifested once more!*

Since (according to that author) *"God's holy presence* that accompanied them was withdrawn,"* perhaps we should search the Scriptures for the return of that *holy* presence. If it is *rediscovered,* we might once again see the miracles and mighty works which the author claims vanished along with it! An awesome quest of this magnitude will surely consume a great deal of time—so please bear with me as we begin. I assure you that the outcome of our search will be well worth your while.

One of the first mentions of the word *holy* in the New Testament was in reference to Jesus:

> And the angel answered and said to her, "...the *Holy* Spirit will come upon you, and the power of the Most High will overshadow you; and for that reason the *holy* offspring shall be called *the Son of God.*" (Luke 1:35; emphasis mine.)

In Revelation, the last book of the Bible, He was still called *holy:*

> ...He who is *holy*...says this.... (Rev. 3:7b; emphasis mine.)

John the Baptist's pronouncement concerning Jesus' ministry had to do with the Advent of God's *Holy* Spirit:

> As for me, I baptize you in water for repentance, but He who is coming after me is mightier than I, and I am not even fit to remove His sandals;*He Himself will baptize you with the Holy Spirit and fire.* (Matt. 3:11; emphasis mine.)

Well, so far so good. At least now we know that to *whatever* place the *holy* presence had been withdrawn—it *returned* and *resided* within Jesus; and He promised to do something *very* special with it!

> And I will ask the Father, and He will give you *another Helper,* that He may be with you forever; *that is the Spirit of truth...*He abides *with* you, and will be *in* you. (Jn. 14:16,17a,c; emphasis mine.)

The great emphasis in that chapter is that Jesus would soon be leaving His disciples—but not abandoning them! He would send them *another* Helper, the *Holy* Spirit, who until then had only been *with* them but would soon be *in* them. The word for "another" in the Greek carries with it the thought of "another *of the same kind.*" In verse eighteen Jesus elucidated what He meant quite clearly:

> I will not leave you as orphans; *I will come to you.* (Emphasis mine.)

It is evident that Jesus intended to return to His disciples in the Person of the *Holy* Spirit; thus fulfilling the prophetic words of John the Baptist when he said that Jesus would baptize believers with the *Holy* Ghost. Jesus reiterated this promise in Luke 24:49 just prior to His ascension into heaven:

> And behold, I am sending forth the promise of My Father upon you; (the *Holy* Spirit, ed.) but you are to stay in the city until you are clothed with *power* from on high. (Emphasis mine.)

In the Book of Acts Luke expands upon Jesus' last words thusly:

> But you shall receive *power* when the *Holy* Spirit has come upon you.... (Acts 1:8a; emphasis mine.)

It was an absolutely established fact in the mind of Jesus, that the *Holy* Spirit was to be sent to and received by His disciples, and that He would be accompanied by *power* that would produce *signs, wonders and miracles!* Such was the case at the *Holy* Spirit's Advent on the Day of Pentecost when the *miracle* of "speaking with other tongues" was experienced by at least 120 people:

> And there appeared to them *tongues as of fire* distributing themselves, and they rested on each one of them. And they were *all filled with the Holy Spirit and began to speak with other tongues,* as the Spirit was giving them utterance. (Acts 2:3,4; emphasis mine.)

The book of Acts is replete with miracles and mighty works of power which were wrought not only by Apostles, but also by elders and deacons; so it would seem safe to conclude that the *HOLY PRESENCE had returned!* Of course it might yet be argued that the gift of the *Holy* Spirit was only for the Apostolic Age; after which the *HOLY PRESENCE* was withdrawn again. Let's lay that old wives' tale to rest with God's promise from Peter's sermon, preached on the Day of Pentecost:

> ...Repent, and let each of you be baptized in the name of Jesus Christ for the forgiveness of your sins; and you shall receive the gift of the *Holy* Spirit. *For the promise is for you and your children, and for all who are far off, AS MANY AS THE LORD OUR GOD SHALL CALL TO HIMSELF.* (Acts 2:38,39; emphasis mine.)

In the Old Testament the Tabernacle and later Solomon's Temple were the center of worship in Israel and it pleased God to manifest His *HOLY PRESENCE* there. The attention of the whole nation focused on that sacred spot, knowing that God's *Holy* Spirit hovered over the *Holy* of holies. If you could have asked anyone in those days where God's *HOLY PRESENCE* might be found, the answer would have been given without hesitation—*"In the Temple!"* Yet, the Bible clearly teaches:

> ...The Most High does not *dwell* (abide *permanently,* ed.) in houses (temples) made by human hands.... (Acts 7:48a; emphasis mine.)

The Temple of the Old Testament was merely a type or a shadow of God's ultimate plan to place His *HOLY PRESENCE* in a temple eclipsing anything that even Solomon in all his glory could provide! Someday there would be no more temple of stone and gold to house God's *HOLY* PRESENCE—He had planned something *far* superior. Ultimately He would encase His *HOLY PRESENCE* in flesh—He would dwell in His own creation, *man.*

This actually began to take place resurrection Sunday evening when:

> Jesus therefore said to them again, "Peace be with you; as the Father has sent Me, I also send you." And when He had said this, He *breathed* on them, and said to them, "Receive the *Holy* Spirit." (Jn. 20:21,22; emphasis mine.)

The phrase, "receive the *Holy* Spirit" is in the imperative *present tense*, signifying that Jesus was bestowing the *Holy* Spirit to His disciples *at that moment;* but for what *purpose?* That purpose is contained in the previous phrase, "as the Father has sent Me...." which means "in the same manner." Jesus commissioned *us* with the *same* power and authority over Satan that *He* had. Buried within that statement is a far more profound meaning which when comprehended, will produce the same works of power that Jesus manifested.

Under the Old Covenant the *HOLY PRESENCE* was primarily confined to the Temple, occasionally descending upon a prophet, priest or king for a specific task and then departing. In this timeframe the *Holy* Spirit never *remained* upon anyone permanently.

John the Baptist came as a forerunner of the Messiah and announced that He was at hand. Yet one major question kept recurring in his mind: "How will I recognize Him when He arrives?" The answer was profoundly simple:

> And John bore witness saying, "I have beheld the Spirit descending as a dove out of heaven; and He *remained* upon Him. And I did not recognize Him, but He who sent me to baptize in water said to me, 'He upon whom you see the Spirit descending and *remaining* upon Him, this is the one who baptizes in the *Holy* Spirit.' And I have seen, and have borne witness that *this is the Son of God.* " (Jn. 1:32-34; emphasis mine.)

The one *unmistakable* sign of recognition that God gave to John was, "He upon whom you see the Spirit descending and *remaining* upon Him, this is the one...." That sign was confirmed in the Person of Jesus Christ! Never in the annals of history had the *HOLY PRESENCE* ever *remained* upon any prophet, priest or king; but this man held all *three* offices— He was **Prophet, Priest *and* King!**

It was obvious that God was beginning to do something new in the earth; He had taken up residency in a *person.* Jesus, therefore, had become the first **LIVING TEMPLE!** God could now live His life in and through Jesus—His hands were now the hands of God; His feet were the feet of God; His eyes were the eyes of God; His mouth was the mouth of God; and His mind was the mind of God. Is it any wonder then, that it was said of Christ:

> For it was the Father's good pleasure for *all* the *fullness* to *dwell* in Him.

and

For in Him *all* the *fullness of Deity dwells in bodily form.* (Col. 1:19; 2:9; emphasis mine.)

These would be no more than grandiose statements of religious pomposity if they were not *confirmed* by the *miracles, signs, wonders and mighty works* which accompanied the life and ministry of Jesus everywhere He went. The sick were healed; lepers were cleansed; the secrets of men's hearts were revealed; the hungry were fed miraculously and the dead were raised—these were but a few of the *credentials* of this *LIVING TEMPLE* in whom the *HOLY PRESENCE* dwelled!

After John the Baptist had been thrown into prison he began to have questions whether or not Jesus was the promised Messiah; so he sent two disciples to Jesus, asking, "Are You the One who is coming, or do we look for someone else?" (Matt. 11:3)

The most effortless reply would have been a simple, "Yes, I am; you need not look for someone else!" But that was *not* Jesus' response at all. He detained John's disciples for *hours* while He held a healing and deliverance service. Let's read the account:

> At that very time He cured *many* people of diseases and afflictions and evil spirits; and He granted sight to *many* who were blind. And He answered and said to them, *"Go and report to John what you have seen and heard: the blind receive sight, the lame walk, the lepers are cleansed and the deaf hear, the dead are raised up, the poor have the gospel preached to them. And blessed is he who keeps from stumbling over Me."* (Luke 7:18-23; emphasis mine.)

Why did Jesus go to such elaborate lengths to relay that *cryptic* reply to John, instead of giving the less complex answer suggested earlier? To answer this we must first be reminded of the sign God had given John by which he might recognize the Messiah:

> ...He upon whom you see the Spirit descending and *remaining* upon Him, this is the one.... (Jn. 1:33b; emphasis mine.)

Through this display of kingdom authority (the working of signs, wonders, miracles, and mighty works of power) Jesus was saying to John, "The *HOLY PRESENCE* is *still* resident within Me! I am *still* God's *LIVING* TEMPLE—the anointing has not been rescinded. By these signs you will know that *I AM HE!*" Plain and simple—*that* was the message to John.

How do *we* respond when confronted by the world with a paraphrase of John's question: "Is He the One who was coming, *or do we look for someone else?*"

Do we....

   — 1.   Explain that Jesus and the Bible need no *proof.*
   — 2.   Tell them to simply *believe.*
   — 3.   Quote Christian authors.
   — 4.   Tell them to enroll in a Bible class.
   — 5.   Give them Christian books to read.
   — 6.   Refer them to *Schofield's notes.*
   — 7.   Quote *"Larkin's Dispensational Truth."*
   — 8.   Quote your denominational "statement of faith."
   — 9.   Explain what "mainstream denominations" believe.
  —10.   Refer them to your pastor.
  —11.   All of the above.
  ✓12.   *None* of the above.
  ✓13.   *Other: Show* them as *He* did—*by miracles and signs!*

O, that the church would stop excusing its lack of power and rise up in *demonstration* of the *Holy* Spirit—performing the same mighty works of the kingdom that Jesus did! The same *HOLY PRESENCE* that made Jesus a *LIVING* TEMPLE now resides in the church, which is *His body.*

> Do you not know that you are a *temple of God,* and that *the Spirit of God dwells in you?*...for the *temple of God* is *holy* and *that is what you are.*

> Or do you not know that your body is a **temple of the** *Holy Spirit who is in you,* whom you have from God...

> ...for *we* are the **temple of the living God...**

> So then you are no longer strangers and aliens, but you are fellow-citizens with the saints, and are of *God's household,* having been built upon the foundation of the apostles and prophets, Christ Jesus Himself being the corner stone, in whom the whole building, being fitted together is growing into a *holy temple* in the Lord; in

whom *you also are being built together into a dwelling of God in the Spirit.* (I Cor. 3:16,17b; 6:19; II Cor. 6:16; Eph. 2:21; emphasis mine.)

The *HOLY PRESENCE* that *returned in Christ is now resident in his body the church!* If the "withdrawing of the *HOLY PRESENCE*" was the cause for miracles to become "few and far between," (as that author claims), then we may safely conclude that the *return* of the *HOLY PRESENCE* would *initiate* mighty works of signs, wonders and miracles—and that is exactly what is happening today. The fact that some people stumble blindly over miracles without even recognizing them is not cause for saying, as the author alleges, that they are "few and far between." Jesus said:

Truly, truly, I say to you, he who believes in Me, *the works that I do shall he do also; and greater works than these shall he do;* because I go to the Father. (Jn. 14:12; emphasis mine.)

Please read: Ephesians 3:19; 4:13; Colossians 1:19; 2:9 and lastly, read Paul's prayer for the Ephesian church *which is also my prayer for you....* (Eph. 1:16-23)

The Subtle Seduction *Exposed!*

The *subtle seduction* woven throughout both books is that miracles are not needed in the church today. He claims on occasion to believe in miracles but the *overwhelming negativity* heaped upon anything even *remotely* related to signs, wonders or miracles betrays his *true* sentiments! To illustrate my contention, he states:

Paul declared that **"the power"** is in the **preaching of the cross.** Even in the book of Acts there were instances of powerful gospel preaching with many pagans converted (Paul *"so spoke* that a great multitude...believed...."* Acts 14:1) **without any miracles being performed. There were other occasions when great miracles occurred, yet the crowd's reaction was to beat and imprison Paul and his companions, or force them to flee.**[5] (Italics in the original, bold highlights mine.)

People are often won to Christ without any visible miracle occurring other than that of the Holy Spirit's convicting power. Who among we

Full Gospel believers would debate that? Our Scriptural argument is that there *are* times when miracles are *absolutely imperative* to convince unbelievers. This was evidenced in the ministry of our Lord and throughout the early church.

Since the author's argument hinges upon Acts 14, verse one, let us examine the verses that follow:

> But the Jews who disbelieved stirred up the minds of the Gentiles, and embittered them against the brethren. Therefore they spent a long time there speaking boldly with reliance upon the Lord, *who was bearing witness to the word of His grace, granting that signs and wonders be done by their hands.* But the multitude of the city was divided; and some sided with the Jews, and some with the apostles. (Acts 14:2-4; emphasis mine.)

It is interesting to note the author chose verse 1 to illustrate his contention that *"preaching* without miracles is *all* that is necessary."* At the same time he makes light of miracles alluding to times when, following great miracles the crowd's reaction was antagonistic toward the apostles. Need he be reminded of several similar occurrences of hostile rejection which followed the preaching of the Word, even when *no* miracles had been performed! The intimation seems to be; "miracles really don't serve much purpose today, because in the past they and those who performed them were *sometimes* rejected by the people." That was *often* the case in Jesus' life also—would the author then make light of *His* ministry? The reactions of people neither endorse nor negate *any* facet of the Word of God.

Please note in verse 2 that the resentment against the apostles follows *immediately* after the author's "proof-text" that *miracles* cause persecutions. In this case the resentment followed the *preaching.* Continuing in verse 3, we read "therefore" (or "because of" the persecution which arose over the *preaching* of the word), they spent a long time there." Only now their *preaching* had added impetus: "...the Lord...was *bearing witness to the word...granting that signs and wonders* be done by their hands." Because of the bitter resentments displayed by the townspeople, God determined that preaching alone was insufficient. May I remind the author that it was *God* who "was *bearing witness to the word of His grace, granting that signs and wonders be done by their hands.* "Yet even with a divine endorsement such as that there were yet those who *chose not to believe.* May we never be that *narrow-minded* or fail to read in the context; *"some* (sided) with the apostles."* Those people were converted despite the persecutions, because of *preaching...preaching with signs and wonders following!*

His Major Delusion...*Is* A Major Delusion

Rampant throughout both books in question is the *true* "seduction of Christianity" as readers are *subtly led to disdain anything supernatural.* I submit yet another *seductive* quote:

> The **overemphasis** upon healing and miracles has given birth to **one of the major delusions of our time**...that most if not all sceptics would be convinced if only they could see some *genuine miracles.* This is however clearly not the case. *It is a grave mistake to conclude that God's truth lacks convicting power that only miracles can supply.*[6] (Emphasis mine.)

I have preached the Full Gospel message for 30 years and I have never seen the "major delusion" referred to by that author! Over the years I *have* seen a few scattered individuals who were of the opinion that all sceptics would be convinced if they saw a genuine miracle. Those were almost always new converts who were overly zealous but not knowledgeable in the Scriptures. The meager minority who are thus disposed *hardly* constitutes a "major delusion."

How did the author arrive at the *non-biblical* conclusion that "It is a *grave mistake* to conclude that God's truth lacks convicting power *that only miracles can supply?"* If God's truth has (intrinsically) *all* the convicting power necessary to lead *all* men to Christ then why does the Bible declare: "And they went out and preached everywhere, while the Lord worked with them, and *confirmed the word by the signs that followed?"* The Greek word for "confirmed" means "firm or sure; of force; steadfast; *to stabilitate; basality."* Basality means, "of or at the base; *forming the base;* fundamental—*basic"*; thus indicating that miracles actually form the *base* of, *prove,* and *give stability to* the Word of God! That makes scriptural sense since *miracles are works of the Holy Spirit* and are as much a part of God as is His Word.

> ...The Lord, who was *bearing witness* to the word...*granting that signs and wonders be done by their hands.* (Acts 14:3b; emphasis mine.)

How shall we escape if we neglect so great a *salvation?* After it was at the first spoken through the Lord, it was *confirmed to us* by those who heard, *God also bearing witness* with them, both by *signs and wonders* and by various *miracles* and by *gifts of the Holy Spirit...* (Hebrews 2:3,4; emphasis mine.)

Whose Error Is It?

We must consider the *grave* charge leveled by that author:

> Those in charge of Christian media who promote this **pseudospirituality** must take much of the responsibility for popularizing **the error that** *signs and wonders* **are essential to a full proclamation of the gospel.** In contrast, Scripture clearly says: "For I am not ashamed of the Gospel, for it is the power of God for salvation to everyone who believes, to the Jew first and also to the Greek." (Rom. 1:16) "The preaching of the cross is 'to them that perish foolishness; but unto us which are **saved** it is the power of God...." "It pleased God by the foolishness of preaching to **save** them that believe." (I Cor. 1:18,21)[7] (Italics in the original, bold highlights mine.)

The author contends that it is not only an "error" but "pseudo (false) spirituality" to believe that "signs and wonders are essential to a full proclamation of the gospel," and for "proof" he quotes the aforementioned three verses. No one with even a modicum of spiritual insight would deny either the awesome power of the cross or the absolute *necessity* of preaching the word. (Rom. 1:16; 10:8-17) The Bible does bear out however, that the cross is not God's *ONLY* power. Some other Scriptural designations of God's power are: Acts 1:8; Rom. 1:16; 15:19; I Cor. 1:18,24; Phil. 3:10; Heb. 1:3; II Pet. 1:3. These Scriptures declare that the Holy Spirit; the gospel; *signs and wonders* the cross; Christ; Christ's resurrection; God's words and God's divinity are *equally* the "power of God." Please note that *signs and wonders* are included in that list.

The author decries the belief that signs and wonders are *essential* to a full proclamation of the gospel; in fact he labels such belief as "an error" and "pseudospirituality." The apostle Paul obviously never read his books since he clearly believed that to "fully preach the gospel" included moving in the power of the Spirit *performing signs and wonders.* Thus he wrote:

> *In the power of signs and wonders, in the power of the Spirit*...from Jerusalem and round about as far as Illyricum I have *fully preached* the gospel of Christ. (Rom. 15:19; emphasis mine.)

In order to comprehend what comprises a "full proclamation of the *gospel*" we must have an understanding of the Greek meaning for the words "saved, salvation" and "gospel."

Since the author quoted Romans 1:16 as his "proof-text" let's examine that verse first. Paul says that he is "...not ashamed of the *gospel,* for it is the power of God for *salvation....*" The word used here for "salvation" is *soteria,* which means "rescue or safety (*physically* or morally), *deliver, health,* salvation." (Emphasis mine.) The word for "saved" is *sozo* which means "to save, i.e. *deliver* or *protect, heal, preserve,* save, *make whole."* (Emphasis mine.) *Both* words encompass the meaning of *absolute deliverance,* not *only* from *sin* but also from *sickness and demonic power!*

That author has committed a **grave error** in failing to realize that, according to the Bible, to be "saved" is not *limited* to merely being rescued from hell *but encompasses deliverance, physical safety, health, protection, preservation and for the whole man to be made whole!* Now it becomes clear why, after Jesus performed physical miracles of healing, He often remarked, "Your faith has *SAVED* you." (See: Matt. 9:27-29; Mk. 5:25-34; 10:46-52; Luke 8:48; 17:19; 18:42.) I'm glad the salvation Jesus provided for us is so much *more* than just a "divine fire escape" from hell! We clearly understand that both the cross *and* the gospel are indeed the "power of God for salvation," only now we perceive the full *Biblical* meaning of "salvation" and *all* that it encompasses.

Want Some Good News?

The word "gospel" as many have thought, does not simply mean "you must be born again." Jesus *never* preached the "gospel of *salvation*" He preached the "gospel of the *kingdom*":

> And Jesus was...**proclaiming the gospel of the** *kingdom, and healing* every kind of disease and every kind of sickness among the people. (Matt. 4:23; emphasis mine.)

And Jesus was going about all the cities and the villages, **teaching...and proclaiming the** *kingdom, and healing* every kind of disease and every kind of sickness. (Matt. 9:35; emphasis mine.)

Jesus said, "And **this gospel of the** *kingdom* **shall be preached in the whole world** (not *just* to Israel, ed.) for a witness to all the nations, and *then* the end shall come." (Matt. 24:14; emphasis mine.)

...Jesus came into Galilee, **preaching the gospel of God,** and saying, "The time is fulfilled and **the** *kingdom* **of God is at hand**; repent and believe in the **gospel**." (Mk. 1:14b, 15; emphasis mine.)

The Greek word for "gospel" simply means *good news*, and when we accepted Jesus' atoning work of Calvary and discovered that our sins were washed away that certainly was *good news*. But it is a serious misconception to confine the scope of Jesus' gospel to the removal of one's sins, for all the monumental importance of that act. I rejoice in the knowledge that the Bible encompasses *so* much more *good news* than that! Pity the poor person whose *good news* is curtailed because no one ever informed him of all that his "salvation" includes!

"Salvation" or "to be saved" means:
1. **To be rescued** which is "good news."
2. **To have physical safety** which is "good news."
3. **To be delivered from evil bondage** which is "good news."
4. **To have good health** which is "good news."
5. **To be divinely protected** which is "good news."
6. **To be healed when ill** which is "good news."
7. **To be saved from your enemies** which is "good news."
8. **To be made whole** which is "good news."

These are only a *small* representation of the *GOOD NEWS* you will discover in the *gospel*. Space will not permit more than a cursory mention of the *good news*: we have been delivered *out* of the kingdom of *darkness* and *into* the kingdom of *light;* we have been given the baptism in the Holy Spirit; the gifts of the Holy Spirit; fruit of the Holy Spirit...ad infinitum! The *good news* goes on and on.

Jesus had so much *good news* to proclaim that it took a whole *kingdom* to encompass it. He preached the *gospel (good news,* ed.) of the *kingdom*. Notice in Jesus' proclamations about the gospel of the kingdom, how often they were accompanied by the words **"and healing every kind of disease and every kind of sickness among the people."** It would seem that miracles are an integral part of His "gospel of the kingdom"...**AND THAT SOUNDS LIKE "GOOD NEWS" TO ME!**

Mr. Author...Please *Do* As You *Say*

> It is *absolutely necessary* to allow the **Bible** to judge **every** experience.[8] (Emphasis mine.)

How can the person who made such a definitive statement, go on to quote *prolifically* from other authors (most, if not all of whom are definitely not Pentecostal) and echo the "mainstream church" *repeatedly?* In his books *these, far more often than the Bible,* are the "judges" of experience. So he *says* one thing while he *does* another.

What "Church" Has *He* Been Hanging Around?

> The idea that *"power evangelism"* requires miracles has not been the understanding or the emphasis of the church in the past.[9] (Emphasis mine.)

What "church" has not had this understanding nor emphasis? Most likely it is one or all of the "mainstream denominations" he quotes from so often, *all* of which at one time or another have fought Pentecostal doctrine. He certainly can't be alluding to the Ante Nicene Church (before 325 A.D.) since *they* continually experienced supernatural healings, signs, wonders, and miracles as emphasized by Christ Himself! Let us look to the testimony of Irenaeus, an early church father (130-200 A.D.) who, in a defense of *true Christianity* wrote a book entitled, "Against Heresies." In his era many had already departed from the true faith of the Word of God, espousing the *heresy* that *supernatural signs were no longer required*. Irenaeus responded to this *true heresy* thusly:

> **Wherefore, also,** *those who are in truth His disciples,* **receiving grace from Him,** *do in His name perform miracles,* **so as to promote the welfare of other men, according to the gift which each has received from Him.** **For** *some do certainly and truly drive out devils, so that those who have thus been cleansed from evil spirits frequently believe in Christ, and join themselves to the church. Others have foreknowledge of things to come: they see visions, and utter prophetic expressions. Others still, heal the sick by laying their hands upon them, and they are made whole. Yea, moreover, as I have said, the dead even have been raised up, and remained among us for many years.* **And what shall I more say? It is not**

possible to name the number of the gifts which the church, scattered throughout the whole world, has received from God, in the name of Jesus Christ...calling upon the name of our Lord Jesus Christ, *she* (the church, ed.) *has been accustomed to work miracles for the advantage of mankind, and not to lead them into error.*[10] (Emphasis mine.)

The entire emphasis of Irenaeus is: **one sign of a *true heretic* is his denial that supernatural signs are resident in the church.** Conversely, signs, wonders and miracles are a (super)natural function in the lives of true believers. On this fact the early church fathers were in total agreement!

Further, that author cannot claim to be representing the major Pentecostal denominations of today. May I quote some official statements of doctrinal position concerning healing/miracles:

The Assemblies of God:

> *Divine healing is an integral part of the gospel. Deliverance from sickness is provided for in the atonement, and is the privilege of all believers.* (Isa. 53:4,5; Matt. 8:16,17; Jas. 5:14-16) (*"The Fundamental Truths of the Assemblies of God,"* Article #12. Italics in the original. (bold highlights mine.)

(The word "integral" means, *"necessary to the completeness of the whole; essential."* Simply stated, you cannot remove miracles of healing from the preaching of the gospel and maintain that you have a complete or *full* gospel. Ed. Note.)

The Pentecostal Holiness Church:

> We believe that *provision was made in the atonement for the healing of our bodies* as set forth in the following Scriptures: Isa. 53:4,5; Matt. 8:16,17; Mk. 16:15-18; Jas. 5:14-16; Ex. 15:26, to which we would also add Rom. 8:26-28. And, while we do not condemn the use of medical means in the treatment of physical disease, we do believe in, practice and commend to our people the laying on of hands by the elders or leaders of the church, the anointing with oil in the name of the Lord, the offering of prayer for the healing of the sick. (Page 47 of the 1985 *"Manual of The Pentecostal Holiness Church."* Article #12. Emphasis mine.)

The Open Bible Standard Church:

We believe that divine healing is the power of God to heal the sick and afflicted in answer to believing prayer, *and is provided for in the atonement.* We believe that God is willing to, and does, heal the sick today. Scripture references: Isa. 53:4,5; Matt. 8:16,17; Jas. 5:14-16; Acts 3:16. (Page #9, article "N", *"Policies and Principles."* Emphasis mine.)

The Pentecostal Church of God:

Healing is for the physical ills of the human body and is wrought by the power of God, through the prayer of faith, and by the laying on of hands, (Mk. 16:18; Jas. 5:14,15); *it is provided for in the atonement of Christ,* and is available to all who truly believe. (*"Tenets of Faith"* Article #3, under subheading #12. Emphasis mine.)

The Church of God of Prophecy:

Divine healing provided for all in the atonement. Ps. 103:3; Isa. 53:4,5; Matt. 8:17; Jas. 5:14-16; I Pet. 2:24 (*"1986 Assembly Minutes"* of The Church of God of Prophecy, page 162 under *"Teachings of the Church of God of Prophecy."* Emphasis mine.)

Without exception, five of the leading Pentecostal denominations agree that *"divine healing is provided for in the atonement of Jesus Christ."* Since provision was made in the atonement for physical, mental and emotional healing as well as deliverance from all forms of Satanic oppression, *who* can deny that miracles are an *inseparable* part of the gospel? Briefly reiterating what I wrote earlier; the words used in the Greek for "saved" and "salvation" encompass *total* deliverance from sin, sickness, disease, infirmity, demonic oppression and *all* the works of the enemy. *The work of the cross is a whole work for the whole man!*

*Un*familiarity Breeds Contempt

Since that author makes light of "power evangelism," we must conclude that he is *unfamiliar* with either the Word of God *and/or* the ministries of Jesus and the apostles who *continually* blended their message, ministries and miracles into one outpouring of love and compassion for wounded humanity. How could anyone *remotely* Pentecostal with even a *modicum* of Biblical knowledge have missed the following "power evangelism" Scriptures?:

Matt. 4:23-25; 9:1-8; 9:32,33; 10:7,8; 12:15,22,23; 14:34-36; 15:30-39; 19:2; Mk. 1:30-34, 39-45; 2:1-13; 3:1-11; 6:53-56; 7:31-37; Luke 4:38-42; 5:12-15,17-25; 6:17-19; Jn. 2:23; 6:1-14; 12:9-18; Acts 2:1-12,22, Acts 2:41-44; 3:1-26; 4:4,29-33; 5:1-16; 6:7,8; 8:4-24; 9:32-42; 10:1-48; 13:6-12; 14:1-3; 14:8-11; 15:12; 16:16-34; 19:1-20; 28:1-9; Rom. 15:16-20; I Cor. 2:1-5; 4:19,20; 14:24,25; Heb. 2:1-4

I trust the *"subtle seduction"* of *anti-miraculous, anti-healing, anti-Pentecostal and anti-meditation* doctrines woven throughout his books is now abundantly evident to the reader. In conclusion, it is only fitting that I quote that author once again:

> **How much more essential would public correction be if a modern Hymenaeus or Philetus as a best-selling author...were leading** *millions* **astray!**[11] (Italics in the original, bold highlights mine.)

I couldn't agree more!

Please note: while he quotes liberally from many anti-Pentecostal leaders, "mainstream" churches, demons, spiritists, witchcraft newspapers and the occult to bolster his allegations of "heresy" within the Church; the quotes in this book, with *few* exceptions, *are from apostles, prophets, Jesus and the Word of God.*

May that author be reminded of the counsel of Gamaliel when the apostles were on trial before the Pharisees and Sadducees:

> And so in the present case, I say to you, stay away from these men and let them alone, for if this plan or action should be of men, it will be overthrown; *but if it is from God, you will not be able to overthrow them; or else you may even be found fighting against God.* (Acts 5:38,39; emphasis mine.)

Birds of A Feather...*Flock Together*

There is a denominational Bible Institute (which shall remain nameless) whose doctrinal position has always been *rabidly* anti-

Pentecostal, anti-healing, anti-miraculous, anti-Christian Meditation. Since the outpouring of the Holy Spirit at the turn of the century they have *firmly* maintained the position that the Pentecostal movement is a "cult," which basically means "non-Christian." No book favorable to any Pentecostal doctrine has *ever* been carried by their bookstore. Yet *both* of the books we have just reviewed are not only *prominently* displayed in a large stand-alone bookcase in the store, but are also featured in an impressive *pyramidal display* in the window! Said books seem to be *just* what these anti-Pentecostal people were waiting for, which ought to indicate just how "favorable" to Pentecostal doctrines *they* think his books are! If that Bible Institute relishes his books as "anti-Pentecostal" and "anti-miraculous," then *how should we Pentecostals feel about what he has written?*

I know how *I* feel....

¹ Hunt, Beyond Seduction, p. 3.
² Ibid., p. 106.
³ Hunt, Mc Mahon, The Seduction of Christianity, p. 43.
⁴ Hunt, Beyond Seduction, p. 75.
⁵ Ibid., p. 78.
⁶ Ibid., p. 104.
⁷ Ibid., pp. 77,78.
⁸ Hunt, Mc Mahon, The Seduction of Christianity, p. 179.
⁹ Hunt, Beyond Seduction, p. 78.
¹⁰ Edited by Reverend Alexander Roberts and James Donaldson, Translation of the Writings of the Fathers, Ante-Nicene Christian Library, Vol. 5, Irenaeus, Vol. 1, (Edinburgh, T & T Clark, 1868).
¹¹ Hunt, Beyond Seduction, p. 37.

5

CHRISTIAN MEDITATION

An Explanation

Throughout the remainder of this book you will notice that I refer to regenerated man's spirit as "(S)spirit." We read in Scripture, "But he that is joined unto the Lord is *one spirit.*" (I Cor. 6:17; emphasis mine.) There is an absolute merging of the two spirits—God's and man's and they become one. Thus, when we enter the realm of our (S)spirit we are in essence moving into the dimension of the Holy Spirit who has united Himself to us. A more in-depth definition of this subject will be given later in the book.

It is a fact of Scripture—the gifts of the Holy Spirit still exist, and they should be functional in the church of today! Perhaps at some time you have served as a channel through whom the Holy Spirit manifested His presence by means of supernatural gifts. This is an indication that at that moment you were in tune with His program. But how was that accomplished? Could you describe in detail what caused that display of a divine gift? I doubt it, since for most people these things simply *happen* with no apparent *cause.*

But there *was* a cause, even though most of us have gone through life being unaware of it—seeing only the effect, that is, a gift of the Holy Spirit, vision, dream, etc.

It is the distinct and stated purpose of this book to examine the Scriptural means at our disposal by which we may enter into the realm of (S)spirit. No longer must we be passive onlookers, waiting for something to happen but we can, and should be, active participants in the Divine drama! That is how it was in the early church—people moving in the dimension of (S)spirit, shaking the world with signs, wonders and miracles which accompanied them everywhere. It was even said of them in Acts 17:6 that they "turned the world upside down." Obviously the church of the Twentieth Century bears little resemblance to the church of the First Century in this regard!

Yet, we maintain that Christ is in His church just as He was in the first century and we steadfastly adhere to Hebrews 13:8 which clearly states that "Jesus Christ is the same yesterday and today and forever." Either our theology is wrong or we have missed something somewhere! It is my contention that the latter statement is true, and throughout this book we will be discovering how *very* much we have missed and how it has adversely affected the church. Many obstacles have prevented us from entering in to the rich anointing that brings forth the moving of the Holy Spirit in great power. Let us consider the first obstacles, the flesh and the mind.

Into The Holy of Holies

We read in Hebrews 9:8:

> The Holy Ghost is signifying this, that the way into the Holiest of all was not yet made manifest, while as the *first* (outer, ed.) tabernacle was yet standing.

The tabernacle was the central location from which God manifested His presence in Israel. It was a tent designed by God, Who gave the blueprint to Moses. This became the focal point of worship as the nation of Israel moved through the wilderness. (When Israel became established in the Promised Land the tabernacle was replaced with Solomon's Temple, the design of which was identical to the tabernacle though much larger and more richly ornamented.)

The tabernacle was a portable building divided into two parts: the holy place and the innermost room (the Holy of holies) where God's presence dwelled. When the tabernacle was in use God's presence in the Holy of holies was manifested outwardly by the hovering presence of a pillar of cloud during the day and a pillar of fire at night. God used the tabernacle as a type, or pattern to illustrate hidden spiritual truths. The fact that man is composed of three parts—body, soul and spirit is illustrated perfectly in the three sections of the tabernacle. The outer court (where the sacrifice for sin was offered) corresponds to the flesh, the holy place, to the soul (or mind) and the Holiest of all, to the (S)spirit.

There can be no doubt concerning the meaning of Hebrews 9:8 when we gain an insight into the two root words in the Greek from which we derive the word "standing" as used in this verse. The first is *scheo,* one of whose meanings is "to hold or reign." The second root word is *stasis* which signifies "an insurrection or a popular uprising." Who can doubt the clear intent that the writer of Hebrews was attempting to convey, that the mind of man has been involved and has reigned in a popular insurrection (or rebellion) against his (S)spirit since the fall in the Garden of Eden!

It is my belief (and that of some leading theologians) that there may have been no oral language in Eden, but that man and woman—as well as man and God—may have communicated on the level of (S)spirit. At this juncture in time man was primarily a (S)spirit living in a body, whereas today the reverse is true. We will discuss this in much greater depth later in this book.

When Satan tempted Eve, and she in turn tempted Adam, it was through a direct appeal to their *minds* (the repository of the will, intellect and the emotions). The sequence of events is recorded in Genesis 3:1-7:

> Now the serpent was more crafty (*skillful in deceiving others*; a talent of the mind, ed.) than any beast of the field which the Lord God had made. And he said to the woman, "Indeed, has God said, 'You shall not eat from any tree of the garden'?" And the woman said to the serpent, "From the fruit of the trees of the garden we may eat; but from the fruit of the tree which is in the middle of the garden, God has said, 'You shall not eat from it or touch it, *lest you die.*'" And the serpent said to the woman, "You shall not die! For God knows that in the day you eat from it your eyes will be opened, and you will be like God, knowing good and evil." When the woman saw that the tree was good for food, and that it was a delight to the eyes, and that the tree was *desirable to make one wise,* she took from its fruit and ate; and she gave also to her husband with her, and he ate. Then the eyes of both of them were opened, and they knew that they were naked; and they sewed fig leaves together and made themselves loin coverings. (Emphasis mine.)

There were two major trees in Eden, one of *life,* the other of *knowledge*—and when given a choice, man chose *knowledge*. It is stated clearly, "When the woman saw that the tree was...desirable to make one *wise*..." Equally clear is the Hebrew word for "wise," *sakal* which means "intelligent" or having to do with the *intellect*. Almighty God considered the tree of the knowledge of good and evil so *dangerous* that He enjoined the couple in Eden not to even *touch* the tree lest they die. In fact, they were warned in Genesis 2:17 "...in the day that you eat from it *you shall surely die*" (Emphasis mine.), and that is exactly what happened the moment they partook.

It would be difficult for us to comprehend how they could have literally (physically) died, when Genesis 5:5 tells us that Adam lived to be 930 years old—unless we understand that the *real* Adam was not the flesh and blood body, but rather the (S)spirit man within. That *(S)spirit* man is who died that fateful day in the garden! Understand also that when God speaks of death, He is not referring to a "cessation of being," but rather separation from God—which is a living death.

So we have now discovered that man's initial rebellion against God was on the level of his soul, or his mind. (It would seem logical that since man's mind is where the rebellion began, that this is the arena in which the battle for the submission of man would take place.) The mind of man rose up in willful insurrection against God's Spirit rule—thus his mind and body now *reigned* over his dead spirit. But now, in Christ, we are told to "...consider yourselves to be dead to sin, but alive to God..." (Rom. 6:11) Through Christ, the (S)spirit has come back from the dead, but the mind and the body have reigned for so long something must be done to remedy the situation and reverse the order, bringing both our mind and body under the direct control of the regenerated (S)spirit. Nothing less than this will suffice! Whenever men of God were anointed with oil in Scripture (a symbol of the Holy Spirit's presence and power) the anointing *always* began with the head— and the pattern remains the same today. (See Leviticus 8:12; Psalm 23:5; 133:2)

As the three-fold nature of man (body, soul and spirit) are analogous to the three sections of the earthly tabernacle, Jesus was a perfect representation of the true tabernacle in heaven. His flesh parallels the outer court, His soul the holy place and His Spirit the Holy of holies. As mentioned earlier, man had alienated himself from God, and the fullness of God's presence was withheld from him. But since that day in Eden God has been *re*revealing Himself to fallen humanity.

In Exodus 26:33 we are told that the veil in the tabernacle would serve as a partition between the holy place and the Holy of holies—a barrier for those not intended to enter into or experience the presence of God. Later in that same book Moses descended from Mount Sinai where he had been in the presence of God and had received the Ten Commandments. His face shone so with the glory of God that the people of Israel were afraid to look upon him, so he veiled his face—once more concealing the presence of God from men. Thus it continued down through the ages—man separated from God's presence, until God bridged that gap in the person of Jesus Christ.

The Bible says that the fullness of God dwelt in Jesus in bodily form (Col. 1:19; 2:9), yet the world did not recognize the Father's presence. When confronted by the Pharisees who had asked belligerently, "...where is Your Father?" Jesus responded by saying, "...you know neither Me, nor My Father; if you knew Me, you would know My Father also." (Jn. 8:19) A similar statement is recorded in John 14:7-11 where Jesus was preparing His disciples for His imminent departure. Jesus said:

> "If you had known Me, you would have known My Father also"...Philip said to Him, "Lord, show us the Father, and it is enough for us." Jesus said to him, "Have I been so long with you, and yet you have not come to know Me, Philip?"

The Father had taken up residence in Jesus, but was veiled by His flesh; a fulfillment of Old Testament typology (see Exodus 26:33). Even those closest to Him didn't recognize the Father within—it even took a divine revelation for Peter to make his declaration of faith in Matthew 16:13-17. This concealment was to terminate at the cross—*the veil would be removed forever!*

As I have said elsewhere, the cross is so much more than a divine "fire escape" to keep us from hell—it is that for which men of all ages have sought—*the unveiling of God's presence.* Cruel hands drove the spikes which held Jesus on the cross that day and thrust the lance upward into His heart. To the executioners it was just another Jew about to die. Little did they realize the important role they were playing in the unfolding of the divine drama. It was far more than simply another Roman execution—as the nails were driven and the spear was thrust, *it was God rending the veil!* (See Heb. 10:19,20.)

> And Jesus cried out again with a loud voice, *"It is finished!"* (John 19:30) and yielded up His spirit. "And behold, the veil of the temple was torn in two *from top to bottom...*" (Matt. 27:50,51a; emphasis mine.)

Notice that the veil of the temple was rent from top to bottom, indicating that the way into the Holy of holies had not been opened by man, but by God Himself. "It is finished" was not a cry of defeat or despair but the grand finale in God's plan to reconcile Adam's fallen race to Him. Even as the veil of the temple (the spiritual analogy) was torn, the veil of His flesh which had hidden the presence of God (His Spirit) in the Holy of holies was now ripped apart, revealing not only the Father's presence but the greatest love of all time. The way into the Holy of holies was now open for all who would accept His sacrifice to personally experience the intimate relationship of the Edenic fellowship as God again began calling for His creation to know Him.

He has now taken up residence within our (S)spirits and longs to walk in intimate fellowship with us there; but Hebrews 9:8 emphasizes that there can be no entrance into the deepest recesses of our (S)spirits (God's Holy of holies within us) until the outer tabernacle of the flesh and soul (mind) is brought to its knees in humble submission to our regenerated (S)spirits. According to the Scriptures this is an *absolute* requirement and not open to disputation!

6

LOOKING INTO THE MYSTERIES

Before proceeding further, please read the second chapter of First Corinthians as well as John 3:1-12. Chapter two of First Corinthians is one of the great expositions on the *mystical* aspects of the Scriptures, as we will soon discover.

The Apostle Paul exclaims in verse one, "...proclaiming to you the testimony of God." The word for "testimony" is also translatable as *mystery*. This rendering not only sheds new light on the verse, but links it textually to other verses in this chapter and elsewhere which refer to God's mysteries.

It is often preached that the Word of God is very simple and easily understood—thus anyone and everyone can *easily* comprehend it. I strongly disagree with this premise! Though Scripture bears out that the way of *salvation* is eminently clear:

> And an highway shall be there, and a way, and it shall be called the way of holiness; the unclean shall not pass over it; but it shall be for those: the wayfaring men, *though fools, should not err therein.* (Isa. 35:8; emphasis mine.)

The way that leads to God is *so* simple, *so* clear, *so* evident that even a fool could not miss it—but what about the *rest* of the Word of God? There is strong evidence that much of the Word's treasures are available only to those who have enough hunger to search for them.

The Apostle Peter wrote, concerning the writings of the Apostle Paul:

> ...As also in all his letters, speaking in them of these things, in which are some things *hard to understand...* (Emphasis mine.)

And hear Paul himself:

> ...But we speak God's wisdom in a *mystery,* the *hidden* wisdom... (Emphasis mine.)

Everywhere we look in the New Testament we discover evidence of those things which God Himself has concealed with a distinct purpose. The words "mystery, mysteries, hid" and "hidden" appear a total of *thirty-eight* times in the New Testament, which would seem strange if it were true that the Bible is a *completely* open book to even the casual observer.

Consider also the numerous parables spoken by Jesus. The words "parable" or "parables" occur no less than *forty-six* times in the Gospels. A parable is an illustrated story—often with a *hidden meaning concealed from the hearers.* Hear Jesus' words in Matthew 13:13, 34, 35:

> Therefore I speak to them in parables; because while seeing they do not see, and while hearing they do not hear, *nor do they understand...*all these things Jesus spoke to the multitudes in parables, and *He was not talking to them without a parable,* so that what was spoken through the prophet might be fulfilled, saying, "I will open my mouth in parables; I will utter things *hidden* since the foundation of the world." (Emphasis mine.)

In Matthew 13:44 Jesus likened the kingdom of heaven to a treasure (something of great value) hidden in a field. He then went on to say that a man, upon discovering said treasure, "...from joy over it he goes and sells all that he has, and buys that field." (Matt. 13:44b) In verse forty-five He gave the anology of a merchant seeking fine pearls who found one of great value and was willing to sell all that he had to possess it. (What value should *we* then ascribe to the kingdom of God?) Since Jesus alluded to His kingdom as "hidden" (concealed), we may conclude that, while salvation is for everyone—the deeper truths of the kingdom are definitely not for just *anyone.* They are certainly not for those who refuse to appreciate their value and/or are unwilling to pay the price to possess them. However, the person willing to seek after God with all of his heart will find that the "hidden treasure" *is* discoverable, and the "pearl of great price" *is* obtainable! But remember, God has said, "And you will seek Me and find Me, when you *search* for Me with *all* your heart." (Jer. 29:13; emphasis mine.)

Whenever mysteries are referred to in the New Testament, it is always with the implication that they are knowable:

> "For nothing is hidden, except to be revealed; nor has anything been secret, but that it should come to light. If any man has ears to hear, let him hear." (Mk. 4:22, 23)

These verses leave no doubt that the desire of God is to unfold His mysteries and make them known, but verse twenty-two explains clearly to whom they may be revealed. It is to the person who has "ears to hear." The Greek word for "hear" is *akouo* and may also be rendered "understand," shedding a slightly different light on what Jesus said—"If any man has ears to understand, let him understand."

Not everyone knows, or desires to know the deeper things of the Holy Spirit as revealed in the Word. There are varying degrees of growth and commitment among Christians, many of whom attempt to get by with a modicum of spiritual effort. These same people read as little of the Word as they feel compelled to do, reading mostly from the Psalms—*because they're short*! Little, if any time is spent in the presence of God in prayer and the in-depth study of His word. These are what I call "Sunday-goin'-to-meetin'" Christians who have little, if any, real experience with the realm of (S)spirit. One purpose for God to conceal deep truths is so that casual observers such as these won't stumble over them by accident. These things are definitely *not* for such people. The Apostle Paul used the word "mystery" in reference to hidden truths when writing to the church at Corinth. This word in the Greek is *musterion* and *W.E. Vine's Expository Dictionary of Greek Words* defines it thusly:

> Primarily that which is known to the *mustes,* the initiated (from *mueo,* to initiate into the mysteries)...In the New Testament it denotes...that which being outside the range of unassisted natural apprehension, *can be made known only by Divine revelation,* and is made known in a manner and at a time appointed by God, and *to those only who are illuminated by His Spirit*...Among the ancient Greeks "the mysteries" were religious rites and ceremonies practiced by secret societies into which any one who so desired might be received. Those who were initiated into these "mysteries" became possessors of certain knowledge, which was not imparted to the uninitiated and were called "the perfected." In I Corinthians 2:6-16 the Apostle Paul has these "mysteries" in mind and presents the gospel in contrast thereto; here "the perfected" are, of course, the *believers, who alone can perceive the things revealed* (Emphasis mine.)

Paul used the term *musterion* to the church at Corinth because he knew they would grasp its deeper meaning. Corinth boasted numerous mystical societies, the hidden secrets of which could be known only to the select few who had been initiated into the inner circle, and whose mysteries were certainly *not* to be known or understood by outsiders.

That is one reason why non-Christians who attempt to read the Bible have such a difficult time understanding it—most of it simply is not written to them. Nominal, immature Christians who seldom open their Bibles and who spend little, if any, time in prayer, find it difficult to understand anything more than basic truths. Deeper mysteries are literally *Greek* to them.

Certainly Jesus confirmed the existence of mysteries in the Word of God. In Matthew 11:25,26 we read:

> At that time Jesus answered and said, "I praise Thee, O Father, Lord of heaven and earth, that *Thou didst hide these things from the wise and intelligent* and didst reveal them unto babes. Yes, Father, for thus it was well-pleasing in Thy sight." (Emphasis mine.)

These verses disclose the fact that it was God Himself Who concealed certain truths, and from *whom* they were hidden—the "wise and intelligent."

The word for "wise" carries one meaning—that of a cunning wisdom akin to that which Lucifer used to deceive the couple in Eden. The word is *sophos*, "to render wise; in a sinister acceptation, to form 'sophisms' (clever, but misleading arguments)."

The word for "intelligent" is *sunetos,* from which we also derive the word *sunesis*, which translated means, "Mentally put together," or the *intellect*. The deeper truths of God's Word are undisclosed to man's intellect because his rational, thinking, analytical mind cannot grasp them. Jesus continued in this vein of thought in Matthew 13:10-17:

> And the disciples came and said to Him, "Why do you speak to them in parables?" And He answered and said to them, "*To you has been granted to know the mysteries of the kingdom of heaven,* but to them it has not been granted. For whoever has, to him shall more be given, and he shall have an abundance; but whoever does not have, even what he has shall be taken away from him. Therefore I speak to them in parables; because while seeing they do not see, and while hearing they do not hear, nor do they understand. And in their case the prophecy of Isaiah is being fulfilled, which says, 'You will keep on hearing, but will not understand; and you will keep on seeing, but will not perceive; for the heart of this people has become dull, and with their ears they scarcely hear, and

they have closed their eyes lest they should see with their eyes, and hear with their ears, and understand with their heart and turn again, and I should heal them.' But blessed are your eyes, because they see; and your ears, because they hear. For truly I say to you, that many prophets and righteous men desired to see what you see, and did not see it; and to hear what you hear, and did not hear it.''

We understand from verse eleven (''To *you* has been granted to know the mysteries of the kingdom of heaven, but to *them* it has not been granted.''), that God allows perception of His mysteries by *some* and *not* by others! Why is it so difficult for many Christians to understand the mysteries of the kingdom? Does God capriciously select certain ones upon whom to bestow this honor, or are names selected randomly in some form of heavenly lottery? The reply to both of the above propositions is a resounding and absolute *NO!* Then what is the answer?

Paul said, in First Corinthians 2:6,7:

Yet we do speak wisdom among those who are mature; a wisdom however, not of this age, nor of the rulers of this age, who are passing away; but *we speak God's wisdom in a mystery,* the *hidden* wisdom, which God predestined before the ages to our glory.

In verse six Paul divulged to whom these hidden mysteries of wisdom were spoken; to ''those who are mature'' or grown up. Numerous Christians (including large numbers who have known the Lord for many years), are still in spiritual diapers and drinking the milk of the Word!

And I, brethren, could not speak to you as to spiritual men, but as to men of flesh, as to babes in Christ. I gave you milk to drink, not solid food; for you were not yet able to receive it. Indeed, even now you are not yet able, for you are still fleshly. (I Cor. 3:1-3a)

Now see what the writer of Hebrews says about this:

Concerning him (Melchizedek, ed.) we have much to say, and it is hard to explain, since you have become dull of hearing. For though by this time you ought to be teachers, you have need again for someone to teach you the elementary principles of the oracles of God, and you have come to need milk and not solid food. For every one who partakes only of milk is not accustomed to the word of righteousness, for he is a babe. But solid food is for the mature, who because of practice have their senses trained to discern good and evil. Therefore ("because of what I have just said," ed.) leaving the elementary teaching about the Christ, let us press on to maturity, not laying again a foundation of repentance from dead works and of faith toward God, of instructions about washings, (baptisms, ed.) and laying on of hands, and the resurrection of the dead, and eternal judgment.

How many deep truths were missed by these poor, immature Christians to whom the Book of Hebrews was written we will never know, since the writer says in verse eleven, "Concerning him we have *much* to say, and *it is hard to explain, since you have become dull of hearing.*"

Barring some physical handicap or some biological or biochemical dysfunction, it is impossible *not* to grow in the physical realm—it is a simple operation of nature—but not so in the realm of (S)spirit, where some even refuse to grow up! In the physical realm growth can be stunted due to neglect, as is sometimes discovered when a child has been kept confined for years in some small enclosure. Mental retardation nearly always develops in such children, and it is much the same in the dimension of (S)spirit—neglect and confinement to the narrow limitations of denominational statements of faith, without searching the Word in the (S)spirit will stunt growth and retard your knowledge of God and His Spirit.

Remember, every denomination has said, in effect, *"Revelation stops here!* We now have more truth than all who were before us. We fought the denominational structures of our forebears because we saw new revelation, but don't you dare to do the same thing!" THAT, MY FRIEND, IS TRUE HERESY AND MUST BE GUARDED AGAINST AT ALL COST! To know—we must grow, and growth will produce its own cycle of knowing and growing until we walk in the revelation-knowledge of the Holy Spirit. Many Christians are physically fully grown, but have (S)spirits which are dwarfed and which are kept from expressing or asserting themselves. The result is spiritual disaster!

7

KEYS OF THE KINGDOM

Jesus declared to Peter, "I will give you the keys (plural, ed.) of the kingdom of heaven..." (Matt. 16:19) Much has been discussed about the possible meanings behind these keys. While I was in deep prayer one day the Holy Spirit spoke clearly to my heart concerning this. He showed me what one—only one—of these keys is. Simply put, it is that there are *key verses of Scripture.* God has not placed these deep truths (which, remember, are not meant for casual observers) in plain view and in consecutive order, point #1, point #2, point #3, etc. Instead, God has scattered various connecting verses throughout His Word. Sometimes they almost seem as though they don't belong where they are, yet like many pieces of a jigsaw puzzle, they await the ones who having "ears to hear what the Spirit says to the church," will assemble them into God's magnificent mosaic of truth.

The assembling always begins with a single spiritual insight into one or more verses which hitherto were unclear. These verses then connect to others (much like individual links), until a chain of truth is forged that cannot be broken.

Jesus said of the lawyers (experts in the Mosaic law):

> Woe to you lawyers! for you have taken away the *key of knowledge*; you did not enter in yourselves, and those who were entering you hindered." (Luke 11:52; emphasis mine.)

This lends strong credence to the fact that one of the "keys of the kingdom" is *knowledge of the Scriptures.* To illustrate how these keys are found and and how they operate, please read Psalm Ninety-one before continuing.

What a magnificent array of promises is contained in this passage: deliverance, covering, and a refuge complete with a shield and a bulwark. There is the promise of angelic protection and long life as well as deliverance from fear, pestilence, destruction and plague. These are powerful promises! How often Christians have quoted these guarantees as though they belonged to them, only to find that the very promises they appropriated didn't work, didn't happen, didn't come to pass—*for them!* Perhaps some of you have been shaken and confused when this has been your experience.

If we are to clarify this situation, it must be clearly understood that the Word of God is not a compilation of magical formulas and incantations that we mumble over and over in the hope that their repetition will somehow help us. (But there is a *key*—and you can and should use it!) Let's examine the key that unlocks the Ninety-first Psalm; the key that opens the door to blessing, health, protection, courage, deliverance, satisfaction and long life. (This key happens to be more easily discovered than some of those leading to deeper truths—and even then most Christians miss it entirely.) The key can be found in verses 1, 9, and 14.

Verse one says, "He who *dwells* (lives, ed.) in the secret place of the most High shall abide under the shadow of the Almighty." Verse nine, "For (because, ed.) you have made the Lord, my refuge, even the most High, your dwelling place." These verses tie in textually with Galatians 5:16 where we are admonished to "walk by (in) the Spirit," and to Colossians 2:6 where we are instructed to, "...so walk in Him."

Examine the foregoing verses also in the light of Romans 8:11:

> "But if the Spirit of Him who raised Jesus from the dead dwells in you, He who raised Christ Jesus from the dead will also give life to your mortal bodies through His Spirit who indwells you."

The third aspect of the key to Psalm Ninety-one is found in verse fourteen, "*Because he has loved Me*, therefore I will deliver him, I will set him on high, because he has known My name." So, it is evident that the promises of Psalm Ninety-one are expressly given *to a particular group of people;* those who "dwell in the secret place of the most High"; those who "have made the Lord their refuge and dwelling place"; and to those who "love Him." Some may conjecture that when it speaks of those who love Him it encompasses *all* Christians—not so! Allow me to remind you of the words of Jesus, Who said, "If you love Me, *keep My commandments*," implying that not all who love Him love Him enough to adhere to all of His teachings.

8

THE WAY TO SPIRITUAL TRUTH

But as it is written, "Eye hath not seen, nor ear heard, neither have entered into the heart of man, the things which God hath prepared for them that love Him." (I Cor. 2:9KJV)

The word for "heart" is *kardia,* from which we get such words as cardiac, etc. Even though we recognize that this word refers to the organ in our chests which we know as the "pump of life," the Word of God uses it in a totally different sense. Whenever "heart" is used in Scripture it always refers to the soul or mind of man. (We will deal more fully with this concept in subsequent chapters.)

Hereafter Or Here-And-Now?

Years ago, growing up in a fundamental denominational church, this verse was interpreted to mean that we would have to wait for all of God's wonders until we got to heaven. Signs, wonders, miracles, healings, and gifts of the Holy Spirit were relegated to the past (which we called "the Apostolic Age") or to the future (in heaven). (It seemed as though our theme song was, "In The Sweet Bye And Bye"—but I'm so glad that I awoke one day to the fact that, in God, there is a *sweet here-and now!*

Closer examination will reveal that this verse has absolutely *nothing* to do with our hereafter in heaven—but has *everything* to do with what God has planned for us in the here-and-now! When Paul spoke of eyes not seeing, ears not hearing and the mind not understanding the mysteries of God, he was not putting these things off to some later date. In fact, he was drawing a very distinct line between the flesh and the (S)spirit of man. He was, in effect, saying that natural eyes, ears and minds cannot comprehend God's plan for the here-and-now! These things can *only* be apprehended by the (S)spirit.

Ever since man's fall in the garden and his resultant separation from God, man has organized religious systems with elaborate ceremonies, rites and rituals filled with pomp and circumstance, in order to once again reach God. In fact, the very first thing fallen man used his newly-acquired intellect for was to form a man-made religion whereby (using fig leaves) he attempted to make his own covering. He knew he was naked and that God required a covering; but the god-man Adam, who had walked in the garden in intimate relationship with his Creator, now had no concept of the Spirit's operation and (relying solely on his rational, thinking, reasoning, intellectual mind) *he immediately arrived at a wrong conclusion!*

Since that hour religions have compiled millions of volumes in the attempt to understand God and His dealings with mankind— and none of these even comes close to sufficing. The simple truth is that Christianity has absolutely, positively and unequivocally, *nothing* to do with religion, and *everything* to do with *relationship!*

You cannot educate God into a person. This book, or the course I teach on *Christian Meditation* and the Renewing of the Mind, are meaningless unless your (S)spirit is open to these truths. Repeatedly we read in Scripture, "He that hath an ear, let him hear what the Spirit says to the church." Since everyone has physical ears, we recognize that He was not speaking of the flesh—rather, "he who has a *spiritual* ear, let him use it to distinguish, listen to, and understand, the voice of the Holy Spirit." The truth that I Corinthians 2:9 is actually attempting to convey to us is that we can never know, or understand things of the Spirit through the use of our five senses, or by carnal understanding.

Man is a tri-partite being, that is, he is spirit, soul and body. His physical body is the repository of the five senses of taste, touch, smelling, hearing and sight, all of which equip him to experience and move about in a physical world. The soul (mind) is the repository of his will, intellect and emotions and enables him to mentally adjust to, evaluate, and cope with his physical surroundings. The soul, as a non-corporeal aspect of his being, also functions as an intermediary between the outer (physical) and the inner (spiritual) realm. (We will cover this in greater depth later.) Then there is his (S)spirit. Actually the (S)spirit is the single most important component of man—for by his (S)spirit, and by his (S)spirit alone is it possible for him to experience God! Only by this medium can he see into the (S)spirit-realm and hear the voice of the Holy Spirit. Is it any wonder then that the Bible says, "Flesh and blood cannot inherit the kingdom of God"? These two, the flesh and the (S)spirit, are diametrically opposed to one another.

> But a natural man does not accept the things of the Spirit of God; for they are foolishness to him, and *he cannot understand them,* because they are *spiritually* appraised (understood, ed.—I Cor. 2:14; emphasis mine.)

The natural man referred to here is not the unregenerate sinner whom we often assume it to mean. The word for "natural" is *psuchikos:*

> *Belonging to the soul (as the lower part of the immaterial in man), natural, physical. It has to do with wisdom springing from the corrupt desires and affections. (W.E. Vine's Expository Dictionary of New Testament Words)*

This is the primary reason why many Christians have great difficulty when it comes to understanding things of the Spirit. The Bible says "...they are *foolishness* to him..." Foolishness means "absurdity, that which is plainly not true or sensible"; in other words, that which is rejected by the senses. The same verse says "...he *cannot* understand them...", so it is no wonder that the natural man struggles so with the "fourth dimension" of the Holy Spirit. The Word of God is absolute on this subject—simply put, he positively, unequivocally *cannot* understand this realm. The natural mind does not have the capacity to "compute" spiritual input!

Things of the (S)spirit do not lend themselves to basic reason, and I Corinthians 2:14 explains why: "...because they are spiritually appraised (understood, ed.)." The greatest obstruction which prevents Christians from walking in the (S)spirit and having an intimate relationship with God is the human mind, or soul. That which was meant to be a *bridge* has now become a *barrier.* Verse nine states emphatically that we cannot know things of the Spirit through our five senses, and although it often does, this need not lead to spiritual frustration. Paul continues, in verses ten through twelve:

> ...for to us God revealed them *through the Spirit*; for the Spirit searches all things, even the *depths* of God. For who among men knows the thoughts of a man except the spirit of man, which is in him? Even so the thoughts of God no one knows except the Spirit of God. Now we have received, not the spirit of the world, but the Spirit who is from God, that we might know the things freely given to us by God... (Emphasis mine.)

We understand from this that these mysteries are revealed to us through *no* other channel than the Holy Spirit.

Paul further said in verse ten that it is "...the Spirit (that) searches all things, even the depths of God." The word for "depths" is *bathos,* which means, "profundity, extent, *mystery*, deep things." This verse links textually with verses six and seven, which say:

> Yet we do speak wisdom among those who are mature; a wisdom, however, not of this age, nor of the rulers of this age, who are passing away; but we speak God's wisdom in a *mystery,* the *hidden* wisdom, which God predestined before the ages to our glory. (Emphasis mine.)

By the above verses we learn that the "depths" of God may only be plumbed by mature believers, who perceive these things in the (S)spirit! Verse eleven makes it evident that the only part of man that truly understands his innermost thoughts and motivations is his (S)spirit. This is followed by:

> Now we have received, not the spirit of the world, but the spirit who is from God, *that we might know the things freely given to us by God.* (Verse twelve)

We are (S)spirit, and as such are privy to the manifold revelations of God, who is also "Spirit." The purpose for receiving the Spirit of God is made evident in verse twelve, "that we might know the things freely given to us by God." Since God created the first man in Eden it has been His desire that His creation would walk with Him in intimate fellowship and that man would be capable of receiving God's revelation-knowledge. Since this transfer of knowledge can only take place in man's (S)spirit, notice the frequent admonitions in Scripture for us to "walk (Greek—live, pitch a tent, ed.) in the spirit." Jesus said of the Spirit:

> But when He, the Spirit of truth, comes, He will guide you into all the truth; for He will not speak on His own initiative, but whatever He hears, He will speak; *and will disclose to you what is to come.* He shall glorify Me; *for He shall take of mine, and shall disclose it to you.* All things that the Father has are mine; therefore I said, that He takes of mine, and will disclose it to you. (Jn. 16:13-15; emphasis mine.)

Where Is God Today?

The church of the First Century knew the power and evidenced the presence of the Holy Spirit through signs, wonders, miracles, visions and revelations, with all nine gifts of the Holy Spirit in operation. The God of the First Century is *also* the God of the Twentieth Century, to which Hebrews 13:8 attests: "Jesus Christ is the same yesterday and today, yes and forever."

The question Gideon asked (when, during perilous times, he was told by an angel that God was with him) is relevant today: "Oh my Lord, if the Lord is with us...*where are all His miracles* which our fathers told us about...?" God never changes, but of course *man* does. The Pentecostal movement was born in the miraculous—that was all we ever knew—but the passage of time takes its toll on people and movements.

Most of our preachers had no formal education in the early days when the Holy Spirit was poured out across America, and our churches were mostly storefront buildings with nothing esthetic to attract people—but our preachers were men of God who knew how to hear from heaven. During the Azusa Street revival in Los Angeles which heralded the outpouring of the Holy Spirit in this century, it was said of the leaders that they would spend hours on their faces, weeping before God, looking to Him for the word to preach, being certain that to miss the mind of the Holy Spirit was to be struck dead. Though I will not attempt to theologically defend such a strong position, I'm convinced there is a certain validity to the sentiment behind it. (I must admit, I prefer that honest, though misguided intensity to the casual, man-made, "sermonettes" delivered by "preacherettes"to "Christianettes," which are so prevalent today!) They certainly carried the credentials of the Holy Spirit—signs, wonders, miracles and healings took place and God honored their simple approach to things of the (S)spirit.

We have come a long way since those "good old days" which few can even remember. Today almost all our preachers have been through college (as I have); some boasting of impressive degrees. Our churches have moved from the other side of the tracks to "Main Street" and we belong to all the right denominational fellowships; but there are few who can say, along with Peter, when he spoke to the lame man at the Beautiful Gate of the temple, "...I do not possess silver and gold, but *what I do have I give to you*: in the name of Jesus Christ the Nazarene—*WALK!*" (Acts 3:1-9; emphasis mine.)

For the sake of clarity, lest I be misunderstood by my ministering brethren, I am not anti-education. Nor am I against building beautiful churches on "Main Street." But these things can never replace the anointing of the Holy Spirit (which often becomes the case); and when intellect and religion are substituted for a revelation/relationship with God we mock the very principles upon which our great movements were founded!

The fact that the present-day church has made intellectual knowledge and spiritual insight an either/or propositions was the recent topic of discussion with several fellow ministers, and we were unanimous that if we had to make a choice between *intellect* or the *anointing of the Holy Spirit* (and I am absolutely convinced that *no* choice is necessary), then we would all opt for the latter. The Apostle Paul had a marvelous blending of both intellect (submitted to the Holy Spirit) and anointing of that same Spirit, which produced signs and wonders.

Today we occasionally see all the gifts of the Holy Spirit in operation, with some people in the church manifesting great ministries. All this is evidence to the fact that God is still moving by His Spirit in supernatural signs, within His Body, the church. But it is my firm conviction that He wants to reveal Himself to the entire Body of Christ in a greater outpouring of His Spirit. We have not yet seen what God has planned for His people—BUT IT IS COMING!

A major purpose for writing this book (and for teaching the same truths in seminars) is to introduce Christians to the realm of the (S)spirit; to instruct them *how to enter* and ultimately *live* in that dimension, as Jesus did.

What do you suppose has kept us from entering into, and consistently moving in that ascendant dimension of the Holy Spirit within us? We now come full-cycle once more to the same conclusion—*our minds.* There is no escaping this one fact—the Scriptures repeatedly emphasize that our minds are distinct *barriers* (when they were meant to be *bridges*) to the dimension of (S)spirit.

> But I am afraid, lest as the serpent deceived Eve by his *craftiness* (the word indicates cunning—the use of his mind, ed.), *your minds should be led astray* from the simplicity and purity of devotion to Christ. (II Cor. 11:3; emphasis mine.)

Satan appealed to Eve's mind and won it over; and ever since that fateful day, men's minds have continued to yield to Satan's influence and have been under his dominion.

9

CONQUERING THE MIND

> For though we walk in the flesh, we do not war according to the flesh, for the weapons of our warfare are not of the flesh, but divinely powerful for the destruction of fortresses. We are *destroying speculations* and every lofty thing raised up against the knowledge of God, and we are *taking every thought captive* to the obedience of Christ. (II Cor. 10:3-5; emphasis mine.)

These are verses filled with great violence. They inform us that we are engaged in spiritual warfare and that our mission is to destroy fortresses—strongholds of the enemy where he has entrenched himself over many centuries. This is lesson number one for babies in Christ who have refused to grow up after years of being Christians: it is time to lay aside the *bottle* and take up the *battle*; to trade *diapers* for the "whole armor of God." Then, fully equipped to fight Satan (and *only* then), we will witness the power of the Holy Spirit in our lives!

Our battle begins in II Corinthians 10:5 with "destroying speculations" or, as the King James Version says, "casting down imaginations." The word for "destroying" means "to demolish with violence," and the word for "speculations" means "to take inventory, conclude, reasoning," from which we derive the English world *logic*.

Have you ever felt an impression that the Holy Spirit was moving upon you to minister supernaturally, and then you *reasoned* whether or not it was possible, *took inventory* of the human, *rational* possibilities of that happening, and then *concluded* that it simply was not plausible? If you can identify with that scenario, then perhaps you can begin to understand why God is so opposed to human intellect (intellect which is not submitted to the Holy Spirit), and wants us to demolish with violence our own reasoning in supernatural affairs! It demonstrates that God is more than *slightly* annoyed at our stubborn persistence in reasoning away His Spirit's *right* to sovereignty in our lives.

The latter part of verse five reads, "...and *we are taking every thought captive* to the obedience of Christ." The word of "thought" is "intellect." There it is again—man's *intellect* getting in the way once more! But that should come as no surprise—ever since Eden it has been that way.

Take note of the important fact that it is not *God* who does the destroying of speculations, or the taking of every thought captive, but it is *we* who are commissioned to do so. This involves a direct act of the will, which initiates the operation of spiritual forces and opens the door for the Holy Spirit to empower us for service.

Throughout the entire human lifetime the mind is subject to programming from one source or another: parents, friends, teachers, television, radio, newscasts, music, books, newspapers, magazines, movies, commercials, billboards, church, the Holy Spirit, Satan, our five senses, clubs, organiations and even the weather—but *most* of all from *ourselves—our own thoughts,"* and the Bible echoes that theme with, "As a man thinketh in his heart, so is he"—or, as the Hebrew says it, "as he reckons in his soul."

A popular theory being expounded today is that a fetus while still in the womb can begin basic education by being talked to with special speakers. The effectiveness of this theory remains to be seen.

Then there is the concept of "genetic memory"; the theory that knowledge possessed by one's forebears can be passed along in D.N.A. and become resident in me now. For instance, I have never taken courses in woodworking, yet I know how to work with wood, and have built almost an entire house, including custom-built kitchen cabinets. A possible (and to me, plausible) explanation for this *unlearned ability* is that knowledge was passed along to me in D.N.A. from my father and his father before him, both of whom were extremely talented in that area; though I didn't *learn* it from him, for he deserted our family when I was a very small child. If there is some validity to the concept of genetic memory then our programming goes back through generations long past. Awesome? *Absolutely!* Regardless of exactly when our programming started, since that time it has been incessant! Much of this programming has been beneficial, but an enormous amount has been extremely detrimental—negative, fearful, harmful, sensual and sinful input, listing only a few on the dark side.

Almost everything we know (or *think* we know) about God has been received through programming—sermons, books, television, radio, friends, etc. Since the Bible instructs us, "...taking every thought captive..." we have our work cut out for us, and *immediately* is not too soon to start! True, the task is monumental—but it *can* and *must* be done.

10

RENEWING OF THE MIND

I urge you therefore, brethren, by the mercies of God, to present your bodies a living and holy sacrifice, acceptable to God, which is your spiritual service of worship. And do not be conformed to this world, *but be transformed by the renewing of your mind....* (Rom. 12:1,2a)

Paul's appeal is that we give our *bodies* to God. I am quite certain that the emphasis here is not so much the rendering of our physical flesh to God, but rather, presenting to Him the repository of our five senses. The analogy is, of course, taken from the Old Testament where the sacrifice offered was slain (no five senses in operation there) and consumed by holy fire, a fire which God Himself sent when the tabernacle was completed.

Paul's further admonition was for believers not to be conformed to this world. "Conformed" means, "fashion or conform self to; to fit into the same mold." Most of the preaching I have heard on this verse has had to do with *physical* conformity: don't wear revealing clothes, don't wear makeup, don't go to movies, don't drink, don't smoke, don't....! In order to join a church you practically had to sign a card, which said, "I won't smoke; I won't chew; and I won't go with girls who do." (I hope you realize that was written with word processor in cheek.)

Please don't misunderstand my making light of so many of the "don'ts" of the church. I am not endorsing any of the things mentioned—neither am I condemning them, they are after all, merely *reflections* of what our *inner man* is really like. I simply do not believe that the church can legislate holiness by changing outward appearances or by dictating what we can or cannot do. That changes no one! What is true is that the church has left its initial calling and has become a *re*former rather than a *trans*former, which reminds me of an amusing story:

A certain fellow who was backslidden more often than not, kept trying to get victory in his life. One night at church he was overheard praying about his sins at the altar. He prayed, "O Lord, clean the cobwebs out of my heart." An elderly sister standing nearby heard him and, laying her hands on his head she prayed, "Don't you do it, Lord—*kill the spider!*"

There is some truly great theology in that simple prayer. What the man prayed for was the removal of the *results* of his actions, much like the man who "sows his wild oats"—and then prays for a "crop failure." What the elderly sister prayed for was the *removal of the source*. As long as the spider lived, cobwebs were certain to reappear; whereas, if the spider died (the source), there simply would be no more cobwebs (the results).

Actually, what are the ways of the world of which we are to beware? They all originate in the *mind* of man: doubts, fears, anxieties, poverty, failure, hatred, gossip, slander—and this is but a small representation of a list which could go on and on. Nowhere in all of God's Word are we ever admonished to be *re*formed, but, rather, to be *trans*formed, and this is a *process* which takes place over a period of time. The word from which we get "transformed" is *metamorphoo*, which means, "metamorphose," a word whose meaning most of us recognize. For illustration, consider the caterpillar—an ugly, green, hairy, creepy, crawly creature with *nothing* esthetic in its favor. It climbs out on a branch and begins spinning a shell (cocoon) around itself, and there, hidden from view, begins going through one of the most remarkable biological changes in nature. After the prescribed passage of time the cocoon shows signs of activity and a new creature comes forth. What emerges is certainly not the ugly, hairy being that went in, but a magnificent, multi-hued butterfly. That is *metamorphoo*—that is *transformation*—and that is what God has called each of *us* to experience. At conversion we become "new creations" as our (S)spirits are re-born, but often the old thought patterns and habits stubbornly remain and cause failure and lack in our Christian walk. Paul says there is a way to overcome through renewing the mind, but the sad fact remains that most Christians are completely in the dark as to *how* to bring this about.

You see, it takes consistent effort (work) over a prolonged period of time, to affect the changes in thought patterns which were programmed into your mind during the course of a whole lifetime. Don't become discouraged if you don't manifest dramatic changes immediately—stay with it and you will soon see marked and permanent change.

Paul explained that this transformation comes about "...by the renewing of your mind...." That word "renewing" has an interesting meaning in the Greek. It literally means "to renovate"—so we are told to affect a *trans*formation by a *renovation* of our minds. Since I am familiar with carpentry, I will use that for an analogy: building new is always easier than renovating. Starting to build from the foundation up allows construction to proceed according to the blueprint, with nothing in the way to prohibit doing just that; whereas *renovation necessitates tearing out the old to make room for the new.* It is always a dirty, aggravating and time-consuming job—but it must be done if the desired change is to take place.

Most of the houses my wife and I have owned have been older ones (the one exception being the house I built), so I've done my share of renovation. The work is backbreaking, with mess everywhere; and it is impossible to fully appreciate all that is involved unless you have been through a similar project. The tearing down seems so unrewarding and unfulfilling—but it is *absolutely necessary!* Then, when the rebuilding process begins, the work of tearing down is appreciated, because the way is cleared for the new construction.

Through *Christian Meditation* the Christian learns how to gain ascendancy over the mind, and bring it under the control of the Holy Spirit. Remember, "casting down imaginations" means to *demolish with violence* an inventory-taking, reasoning, rationalizing, conclusion-making mind! Then begins the *rebuilding* (renovation) of a mind which will be in constant contact with the Holy Spirit—yielded to His every wish, led by and walking in the (S)spirit.

Christians are fond of speculating over D.L. Moody's statement, "The world has yet to see what God could do with a man wholly yielded to Him." I submit that we have *already* seen what God could do with a man wholly yielded to Him—in the person of Jesus Christ! Now we are waiting to see what He could do through a *second* and a *third* and a *thousandth* totally yielded person. *You* could be that individual! The works of power which God performed in the person of Jesus Christ, He will duplicate through *any* Twentieth Century believer who will renew his mind and bring it totally under the Holy Spirit's control.

> Truly, truly, I say to you, he who believes in Me, the works that I do shall he do also; *and greater works than these shall he do;* because I go to the Father. (Jn. 14:12; Jesus; emphasis mine.)

11

THE KINGDOM WITHIN

The Nicodemus Principle

Whenever I speak of the mystical aspects of believers, I sometimes hear remarks similar to these, "But *my* pastor has never taught us anything like this—how come *he* doesn't see it like that?" That is an excellent question, but a difficult one to answer with any degree of certainty, since I probably have never met that person's pastor. Actually, I may have *already* answered it when teaching on the attitudes of the natural mind and its inability to grasp or even see deep spiritual truths.

A portion of Scripture in John 3:1-12 contains the narrative of a nighttime, clandestine meeting between Nicodemus and Jesus. (Please read John 3:1-12 before continuing.) Nicodemus was a Pharisee, a leading religious ruler of the Jews. As such, he was extremely well educated, had a vast knowledge of the Scriptures and was a member of the highest religious tribunal, (the Supreme Court of Israel), the Sanhedren. Yet, for all of this wealth of intellectual knowledge, truths which Jesus considered to be utterly basic for a man of Nicodemus' stature were absolutely beyond his comprehension.

> Nicodemus answered and said to Him, "How can these things be?" Jesus answered and said to him, *"Are you the teacher of Israel, and do not understand these things?"* (John 3:10; emphasis mine.)

Simply because a person has spent many years *intellectually* studying the Scriptures does not mean that his *spirit* is open and receptive to the realm of the Holy Spirit. The "Nicodemus Principle" still holds true today! In the annals of church history we have never had a more intellectually well-equipped clergy—the *LOGISMOS* CLERGY—yet things of the Spirit are largely foreign to them and they *"...cannot understand them, because they are spiritually appraised (understood; I Cor. 2:14b; emphasis mine)."*

Keys To The Kingdom Within

In the first twelve verses of the third chapter of John's Gospel we find keys to the mystical aspects of the kingdom of God. Jesus stated most emphatically:

Truly, truly (or most assuredly, ed.), I say to you, unless one is born again, he cannot *see* the kingdom of God. (verse 3; emphasis mine.)

Countless times this verse has been used to invite the lost to accept Christ, with the meaning given that, "If you are not born again, you can't go to heaven." The Bible *does* teach that we must be born again if we want to go to heaven—but that is *not* the truth that Jesus was setting forth in John 3:3. In order to grasp Jesus' teaching in this passage it is important to understand this one fact: *THE KINGDOM OF GOD IS NOT HEAVEN!* Nothing in Scripture could be plainer than this fact! Heaven is somewhere else—and for some later time, whereas the kingdom of God arrived with Jesus and is for the *here and now.*

The *primary* purpose of Calvary was not to get us out of hell and into heaven. We (not God) have made the cross into a divine "fire escape," with our appeals to "accept Christ so you won't have to burn in hell." While it is true that if you accept Christ as your Savior you *will* escape hell; yet the cross has *far* more significance than that (escape being only a by-product of God's greater plan), and most people miss this point entirely. The crowning reason for Calvary was to bring man back into intimate relationship with God; that we might walk and talk with Him and share in His revelation-knowledge; that the God/man connection of the Garden of Eden might be re-established.

What Jesus very clearly said in John 3:3, is that you must be born again to *see* the kingdom of God. The word for "see" means, "to be aware; know; have knowledge of; behold; perceive." Perceive means, "to take in with the mind, or soul." In John 3:5 Jesus answered Nicodemus:

Truly, truly (most assuredly, ed.), I say to you, unless one is born of water and the Spirit, he cannot *enter* into the kingdom of God (emphasis mine.)

The issue is clearly not one of entering *heaven*—but rather of perceiving and entering the kingdom of God. Well, then, where is this kingdom located, so that we might know more about it?

The kingdom of God cometh not with observation (in the Greek—ocular evidence, ed.). Neither will they say, "Lo here!" or "Lo there!" for, behold, *the kingdom of God is within you.* (Luke 17:20,21; emphasis mine.)

God's *mystical* kingdom exists, hidden away within the deepest recesses of every person. It can't be seen by human eyes, heard by fleshly ears, touched by human hands nor understood by the carnal mind of the natural man. It is man's spirit—a part of God placed withing every infant ever birthed into this world. The Bible teaches that man is made in the image of God: "And God created man in His own image, in the image of God He created him..." (Gen. 1:27)

Have you ever wondered what the image of God in man was? I had pondered that question numerous times during my thirty years of ministry and attempted to comprehend it in the light of my theological training, but I never felt satisfied with the answers. In theology class I had been taught that God was trinity—Father, Son and Holy Spirit and that mas was a tri-partite being—body, soul and spirit; that this similarity was the manner in which God had created man in His own image. Certainly there had to be more to my being *in His image* than that! I felt that someday I would find the explanation—and I did. I found it in the same manner I discovered the material covered in this book: by being absorbed in the Word of God and praying in the (S)spirit. During a session of deep prayer God spoke to me and said, "Would you like to know how I made man in My image?" My reply was instantaneous; "Yes! Of course I would." God continued. "Men have taught that the similarity between a triune God and a tri-partite man is how I made man in My image, but that is not so. When I created the lion, king of the jungle, I gave him no spirit. When I created the eagle, king of the air, I gave him no spirit. To man, and to *man alone* did I impart a *(S)spirit* so that he could know Me intimately and fellowship with Me in that dimension. *That* is how I created man in My image!" God Himself revealed to me that, since He had created a *spirit* being, man was thus enabled to know and experience God's presence.

Before sin entered into man, he had an intimate union with God on a level of (S)spirit which we have never experienced. Every day, in the cool of the evening, Adam walked and communed with God, and God with Him. Only eternity will disclose what innermost secrets God shared with His crowning creation, man! We can only begin to imagine with what joy and anticipation Adam looked forward to his daily rendezvous with his Creator, in fellowship sweeter than honey and more precious than gold!

Then came that fateful day—that awful day when man traded relationship for knowledge; light for darkness; life for death; freedom for bondage; health for sickness; wealth for poverty; gain for loss and joy for sorrow; to name only a few. That was not only the day Adam died, but it was the day when men of all ages died in Adam…"for as in Adam *all die…*" (I Cor. 15:22; emphasis mine.)

That day when God arrived the meeting place was vacant. Adam was nowhere to be found—he was hiding from his God. Never before had there been a reason for Adam to hide from God, but this day he had become a dead man who could not face the Source of all life. God had warned him that, if he partook of, or even *touched* the tree of the knowledge of good and evil, he would die—and *that* death was separation from God! The outer man showed all the normal signs of life but the inner man, the real Adam (the spirit) was dead, separated from his Creator.

When God arrived at the appointed hour, only to discover that Adam was nowhere to be found, in that moment the most plaintive cry of all time went forth through the garden: "Adam, where are you?" That was not a question of location—God knew where Adam was *geographically;* it was an inquiry concerning the *relationship* which had now been severed! That same cry still echoes through the corridors of time, as He continually calls to the hearts of all the fallen sons and daughters of Adam's race—"Where are you?" As I wrote earlier, the grand purpose of the cross was so Jesus could reach up to heaven with one hand and down to fallen, separated man with the other and reunite them in Himself.

Jesus spoke of this when He said:

> But an hour is coming, and now is, when the true worshipers shall worship the Father in spirit and truth; for such people the Father seeks to be His worshipers. *God is spirit;* and those who worship Him must worship in spirit and truth. (Jn. 4:23, 24; emphasis mine.)

His death brought the fulfillment of that promise!

12

FLESH BIRTHS FLESH — SPIRIT BIRTHS SPIRIT

That which is born of the flesh is flesh; and that which is born of the Spirit is spirit. (Jn. 3:6)

Salvation is *three-fold*, and is an *ongoing process!* When you made a decision to accept Christ as your Savior, you probably believed that your entire person was saved. *Not so!* (Perhaps the impact of that statement shocks or offends you. Most new truth has that initial effect upon the hearer, and most of us feel insecurity when old foundations are shaken, however gently. I ask only that you withhold judgment until you understand how this truth develops.) By way of clarification, we need to explore the concept of the three-fold salvation.

Jesus offered more than simply His *body* for our redemption, although that is usually all that is alluded to when we speak of salvation. Since salvation is provided for the whole man, the whole person of Jesus had to be sacrificed. He offered His *body* on the cross for our sins and our sicknesses (I Pet. 2:24); while His *spirit* paid the ultimate price, descending into hell for three days and nights bearing the penalties of our transgressions. (See Matt. 12:40; Acts 2:22-32.) These Scriptures of necessity refer to His spirit, since the body remained in the tomb and the soul does not exist without the body. Mark 10:45b says that Jesus came, "...to give His life *(psuche—soul)* a ransom for many."

So we see that a *three-fold redemption* has been provided for man's body, soul and spirit; however, the three aspects of salvation are not usually *manifested* at the same time. Paul wrote about Christ, "Who *delivered* us from so great a death, and *doth deliver;* in whom we trust that He *will yet deliver* us." (II Cor. 2:10; emphasis mine.) "Who delivered" speaks of a *past* tense, already accomplished salvation; "doth deliver" speaks of a *present* tense, ongoing salvation; "will yet deliver" speaks of a *future*, not yet accomplished salvation. The Word of God is expressly clear on this point—that which is born of God's Spirit is man's *(S)spirit!* Not his body and not his soul (mind)—but his *(S)spirit.*

That is not to say that salvation hasn't been provided for these other aspects of man—it has. But, as we shall discover, it differs from the salvation of (S)spirit. Salvation for the (S)spirit, when received by faith, is instantaneous and perfect. Your (S)spirit at that moment is absolutely prepared for heaven. The body, on the other hand, still goes through the deterioration process of aging as it moves on towards the grave, falling prey to the various ailments which plague mankind.

> And if Christ is in you, though the body is dead because of sin, *yet the spirit is alive* because of righteousness...And not only this, but also we ourselves, having the first fruits of the Spirit, even we ourselves groan within ourselves, waiting eagerly for our adoption as sons, the *redemption of our body.* (Rom. 8:10,23; emphasis mine.)

Though these verses speak of physical death, there is most certainly hope for all who believe! The salvation of the body will be completed at the last trumpet when "the dead in Christ shall rise first." This hope is also stated in I Corinthians 15:21, "For since by a man (Adam, ed.) came death, by a man (Jesus, ed.) also came the resurrection of the dead."

Not only is there a hope of resurrection for believers, but in the meantime there is Divine healing; and for those who have faith to appropriate it, Divine health.

> But if the Spirit of Him who raised Jesus from the dead dwells in you, He who raised Christ Jesus from the dead *will also give life to your mortal bodies through His Spirit who indwells you.* (Rom. 8:11; emphasis mine.)

So, we can clearly see that God has provided salvation for the body, but what about the third salvation—that of the soul? The Apostle James said to Christians:

> Therefore putting aside all filthiness and all that remains of wickedness, (see, *we* are the ones who are instructed to do that, ed.), in humility receive the word implanted, *which is able to save your souls.* (Jas. 1:21; emphasis mine.)

This Scripture gives a clear indication that the soul is still in need of salvation and firmly instructs us as to *our* part in the process. The word "saved" carries with it far greater implications than to merely "escape going to hell someday." The word is *sozo* and means (as explained in depth in an earlier chapter) "deliver or protect, heal, preserve, save, make whole." Philippians 2:12b,13 exhorts us to:

> ...*Work out your own salvation* with fear and trembling; for it is God who is at work in you, both to will and to work for His good pleasure. (emphasis mine)

How can "work out your own salvation" be reconciled with:

> For by grace you have been saved through faith; *and that not of yourselves*, it is the free gift of God; *not as a result of works; that no one should boast*? (Eph. 2:8,9; emphasis mine.)

Yet there is no conflict when man's three-fold salvation is understood. Ephesians 2:8,9 is referring to man's (S)spirit (as evidenced by the preceding verses). In the Philippian reference it is clear that God is already resident in the person spoken of and, since man cannot effect the salvation of his spirit or his body, the salvation alluded to *must be that of the soul*—man's mind.

Whenever God speaks of our minds being changed, it is *we* who are commanded to do whatever is necessary to bring about that change! Why then do we continue struggling in our own strength, hampered with minds that have been conditioned to sin? Repeatedly, we go to the altar in prayer—crying, begging, pleading with God to help us overcome in an area placed squarely within *our* jurisdiction. God will help us, but *we* must do the work! Yet even the work we do is an outcropping of the indwelling Holy Spirit who enables us; "...for it is God who is at work in us...." (Remember, "...the one who joins himself to the Lord *is one spirit*...." (I Cor.6:17; emphasis mine.)

It is absolutely essential that the mind (soul) be renewed. The (S)spirit is the highest aspect of man's being—the *only* part of his being which is capable of having a relationship with the Holy Spirit. Man's flesh, the repository of his five senses, is the lowest facet of his being and allows him to move about in and experience the physical world around him. It would be helpful to envision man's soul as a non-material intermediary (bridge) between the (S)spirit and the flesh. We discussed earlier that one of the major functions of the mind (soul) is the will, and this becomes an extremely important element in our study. Man has the unique ability to make a choice as to which direction he will take—whether to favor the flesh and be of the earth—or to lean in the direction of his (S)spirit, and be spiritual.

Joshua 24:15 relates the challenge of Joshua to the children of Israel: "Choose ye this day whom ye will serve...but as for me and my house we will serve the Lord." So we see that Joshua made a deliberate *choice* by an exercise of his *will*.

Imagine That

One of the key reasons for this book (and my seminars on *Christian Meditation)* is to help Christians learn how to function on the level of (S)spirit instead of the flesh. In order to do this, we must understand the necessity for *re*programming the brain. It ought to be recognized that the brain, our marvelous, God-given "computer" is the physical faculty from which we gain all information regarding the world and self. Since birth, nearly everything you have learned has come to your brain by way of the five senses. Since I dealt with this earlier, I won't belabor the point here. Suffice it to say that the Bible is eminently clear on this, stating emphatically:

> Finally, brethren, whatever is true, whatever is honorable, whatever is right, whatever is pure, whatever is lovely, whatever is of good repute, if there is any excellence and if anything worthy of praise, *let your mind dwell on these things.* The things you have learned and received and heard and seen in me, *practice these things*; and the God of peace shall be with you. (Phil. 4:8,9; emphasis mine.)

One of the key words for meditation in the Old Testament means, "to mutter; say over-and-over again." After all, how are habits formed? Simply be repeating an action or a thought over and over; *practicing* until it becomes "second nature" to us and we are able to perform it without conscious thought. Moral, scriptural habits can and should be formed in the same manner.

Why do you suppose advertisers spend enormous sums of money annually on tricky slogans and catchy tunes that you can't seem to forget? They know if you repeat something often enough, it becomes a part of you—and they believe it enough to spend billions of dollars for just that purpose. They want you talking, or singing to yourself about their product! Again, man has simply discovered something that God has known all along, as many Scriptures relating to meditation in the Old and New Testaments verify.

Since thinking something repetitiously is potent enough to cause a person to change product loyalty, I think it is something *we* as Christians need to know more about. Some of *our* loyalties (priorities) may need to be changed.

The various words for meditation in the Old Testament may be translated thusly: "Converse with oneself, and hence aloud; utter; con-

templation; babbling; reflection; to murmur; ponder; mutter; imagine,"
and in the New Testament the word for "meditate," *meletao* means
"revolve in the mind: imagine."

> *Speaking to yourselves* in Psalms and hymns, and spiritual songs
> (songs in the spirit, ed.), singing and making melody in your heart
> to the Lord." (Eph. 5:19; emphasis mine.)

All of the aforementioned seem to illustrate the Godly use of imagination, with repetition, to bring about a desired spiritual change in the person so engaged. In learning to *re*program ourselves, we will be engaged in
much the same thing, "talking to ourselves"; only now we will be saying
right things, scriptural things, moral things, holy things! Our thought
lives will be filled with God's thoughts, until His thoughts and ours
merge as one with His nature being reproduced in us:

> Seeing that His divine power has granted us everything pertain-
> ing to life and godliness, through the true knowledge ("recogni-
> tion; full discernment"—*not intellectual head knowledge*, ed.) of
> Him who called us by His own glory and excellence. For by these
> He has granted to us His precious and magnificent promises, in
> *order that by them you might become partakers of the divine
> nature*, having escaped the corruption that is in the world by lust.
> (II Pet. 1:3,4; emphasis mine.)

"Mind" Is Not a "Four-Letter Word!"

Occasionally Christians speak about the mind as though it were
something dirty and believe that it has no place concerning things of the
(S)spirit. Some view the mind as a stepchild who is never going to be
quite accepted into the family, when in fact God has strategically placed
the mind as a *bridge* between the flesh and the (S)spirit for a specific purpose. Remember, the mind could not function as it does unless God
Himself had created it that way; so we should not ridicule nor shun its
faculties, among which is the ability to meditate.

13

THE MYSTICAL QUALITY OF BELIEVERS

> The wind blows where it wishes and you hear the sound of it, but do not know where it comes from and where it is going; *so is everyone who is born of the Spirit.* (Jn. 3:8 emphasis mine.)

Note that it does not say, "so is the Spirit of God" (although that is true); it does say, "so is *everyone* who is born of the Spirit." Jesus was saying, "The wind is a *mystery*—coming and going without anyone knowing how, or seeing its source." I am convinced He was saying that those born of the Spirit have a *mystical quality* and, just as the wind is mysterious (the word for spirit and wind in the Greek are *both pneuma*)—so are those born of the Spirit. Don't let the use of the word "mystical" unsettle you. The dictionary definition of mystic is: "person who believes that truth or God can be known through spiritual insight." The word "mystical" is defined as: "having some secret meaning; beyond human understanding; mysterious." Isn't that what we have been maintaining all along—that the mysteries of God are understood outside the realm of human logic?

Those who live in and experience the realm of the (S)spirit are *never* understood by those who do not:

> But as at that time *he who was born according to the flesh persecuted him who was born according to the Spirit*, so it is now also. (Gal. 4:29; emphasis mine.)

But there is a "legitimate" reason why those who live after the flesh do not understand those who live after the (S)spirit. Paul said that the spiritual man

> "...look(s) not at the things which are seen, but at the things which are not seen; for the things which are seen are temporal, *but the things which are not seen are eternal.*" (II Cor. 4:18; emphasis mine.)

This is the place where the natural man has a collision with faith. The Word of God talks about the dimension of (S)spirit, the invisible and the intangible, as though it simply *is*. Since the natural man *cannot* experience this dimension with any of his five physical senses, he rejects it out-of-hand and calls it "nonsense." And for once he is right—the intangibles of (S)spirit are non-*sense*. Of course, if intellect had anything to do with our comprehension of that realm, then a person with even a minimum intelligence would at least *consider* the possibility of its existence.

However, there are elements of the physical world which cannot be discerned by our senses also. For instance, if I told the electric company I wasn't going to pay my bill because I hadn't *seen* any electricity around here all month, wouldn't that be ridiculous? Certainly the electric company would think so! And, of course, it *would* be ludicrous—because no one has *ever* seen electricity. It is invisible—yet only a *fool* would disbelieve its existence, since the dramatic results of electricity can be seen everywhere.

We have all been amazed to see a dog's ears perk up when it hears the "inaudible" sound of a dog whistle, something that the human ear is not capable of receiving. Because people can't hear what the dog hears, does that make the sound any less real? Or does that mean the dog has succumbed to the influence of demons? Of course not! Bees can see ultra-violet light which is outside the human visual spectrum entirely. The fact is that the human eye is comparatively blind, when you consider the vast spectrum of light and realize the infinitesimally *small* portion of it that is visible to man. Again, do we simply "write off" as non-existent all light which the human eye is incapable of receiving (such as ultra-violet, and infra-red, not to mention radio waves—which are also a part of the light spectrum)?

There are voices and pictures passing through the room where you are right now—yet you may be totally unaware of them because your senses are perceiving only silence! You realize, of course, that I am referring to radio and television. If that is true (that the room is filled with voices and pictures), how is it we can't hear or see them? The answer is relatively simple: special equipment is needed to tune in to the particular frequency over which the voices or pictures are being broadcast. Our human senses are simply not capable of being tuned in; so the images/sounds remain in the realm of the invisible/inaudible. The voices and pictures are no less *real,* and no less *there* because you and I can't see or hear them! Our receptivity to them, or lack of it, in no way enhances or diminishes their *reality.*

Crazy—Or Tuned In?

One day, some years ago, I began to hear rock and roll music quite clearly. Since that is definitely not my preference in music, I went throughout the house to locate the source and turn it off. Picture my surprise when no receivers were in use and I still heard the music. Imagine my further consternation when I discovered that no one else heard the music! This happened at least twice more over a period of weeks; once while driving alone in my car. Friends chided me for the "phantom" music that only *I* could hear, and I became somewhat concerned.

Then one day I recalled something I had once read, and rushed off to see a dentist friend of mine. I explained my very real problem to him, half expecting him to smile, if not laugh outright at me. He did neither! After seating me in the chair he simply asked if the music seemed clearer or louder on either side. I replied that it was louder in my left ear. He explained that I was experiencing a rare (but genuine) phenomenon which occurs when a filling in a tooth occasionally reacts to certain acidic conditions in the mouth and performs as a crystal in a crystal radio. In essence, *I had become a radio receiver*. Mystery solved!

The solution was as simple as the problem had been. He touched his drill lightly to each filling on that side of my mouth, explaining that doing so would change the frequency of the *mystery crystal* and thus ended weeks of frustration. The fact remains that *I* heard what I heard—*even if no one else did!* Their not hearing what I heard did not change the reality of it for one moment. Why did *I* hear it, and no one else? Simply because I was "tuned in" to that particular frequency, while those around me were not. The same analogy holds true in the realm of (S)spirit: someone may see a vision, hear the voice of God, or receive a revelation, while others nearby do not, because they are not at that moment sensitive (tuned in) to the (S)spirit realm.

Saul, while on his way to Damascus to persecute the church, was surrounded by a brilliant light and stricken to the ground, at which time he heard the voice of the Lord. The story is recounted in Acts 22:1-11, but for present purposes we will consider only verse nine:

> And they that were with me saw indeed the light, and were afraid; *but they heard not the voice of Him that spoke to me.*

A very similar instance occurred in John 12:27-29:

> ...There came therefore a voice out of heaven: "I have both glorified it, and will glorify it again." The multitude therefore, who stood by and heard it, *were saying that it had thundered*; others were saying, "An angel has spoken to Him." (Emphasis mine.)

Some were tuned in, while others were not! We see this scenario repeated again in the tenth chapter of the Book of Daniel where a breathtaking vision was experienced *only* by the Prophet Daniel, while in the company of others. Please take note of verse seven which says: "Now I Daniel, *alone* saw the vision, *while the men who were with me did not see the vision....*" (Emphasis mine.)

This is yet another instance where an individual with spiritual perception saw into the realm of (S)spirit, while those accompanying him did not.

There are some people who have learned (sometimes by simply stumbling onto it) how to tune in to the realm of (S)spirit, and they see, hear and experience things outside the realm of the five senses. Consequently they are often judged as being abnormal by the natural man, who is often a fine Christian in the same church but who sees with his physical, fleshly, carnal, natural, sensual eyes no farther than the end of his physical, fleshly, carnal, natural, sensual nose!!

Can You Hear The Music?

A friend related to me the story of his aunt, a woman who had served God for many years. As she lay dying, relatives assembled at her bedside awaiting the inevitable. Shortly before the Lord called her home, she began to smile radiantly. Her expression indicated that she was listening but, since no one was speaking, to what or to whom? Then she spoke to those who had gathered around her. "Listen! *Can you hear the music?*" she asked. She then explained that she was listening to a choir singing the praises of God; and shortly thereafter she went home to be with the Lord.

My godmother—a godly woman—had returned home from the hospital after suffering a mild stroke. While waiting to be driven to church one evening, she asked that the Christian radio station be tuned in. Her favorite song was playing, "Some golden daybreak, Jesus will come...." She moved to the edge of her chair and, with rapt expression looked toward the ceiling, raising her arms upward as though embracing someone. Smiling radiantly she said, "O, *don't you see Him?* It's Jesus—He's beautiful!" Having said that, she simply went to be with the Lord who had come to welcome her home.

Deathbed experiences. We can all recount having heard of at least *one* such incident. Many books would not be sufficient to record the true accounts of those who, at the point of death, have seen the Lord, angels or departed loved ones who had come to welcome them into the realm of (S)spirit; or of those who have heard the heavenly choir of the redeemed singing their alleluias to the Savior.

Why do you suppose these incidents so often occur *at or near death's door*? Maybe it is simply God's way of welcoming His children home and nothing more. *Perhaps*. But I believe there is a great deal *more* involved than simply viewing or hearing a heavenly welcoming committee. Let's examine these accounts in the light of some of the facts uncovered in this book.

We have come to recognize that the flesh (our five senses) and the soul (mind, or intellect) are distinct barriers to the dimension of (S)spirit, continually "running interference" to our encountering that realm. The vast majority of Christians make their way through life without *ever* having an awareness that these physical and intellectual roadblocks exist, therefore they do nothing to remedy the situation. Then comes the time when they must die, and many undergo a wonderful deathbed adventure with the unseen realm. Why did that person, who never had a mystical experience in *life*, encounter one at *death*? It is a simple equation—the death of the flesh brings us closer to the realm of (S)spirit. It is not man's (S)spirit or soul that dies—but his body, his flesh, his senses. So, when a person begins the death process his body and mind begin to experience *a diminished awareness of the physical realm,* while his spiritual sensitivities are enhanced. At that moment he sees into, or hears a *dimension that was there all along*—a dimension of which he could have been aware throughout his entire life—a life which is about to terminate momentarily!

What a pity—a life which could have been filled with spiritual insights lived out entirely without ever tasting of heavenly delights until it was too late to turn back the pages of time! That supernatural sphere exists all along—but for most Christians it will take literal death to free them from the physical and intellectual bondage that prevents them from entering it now.

Perhaps Paul is intimating, when he admonishes us to "...*present your bodies* a living...sacrifice...to God..." (Rom. 12:1; emphasis mine.) that there needs to be a "death" of our flesh (senses)—even while we are alive!

The entire history of worship—dating as far back as man's expulsion from Eden—is inextricably linked to sacrifice. If we desire to worship the Father "in spirit and in truth" then our flesh (our senses) must be sacrificed. This effect is achieved best through *Christian Meditation*.

While meditating, the influence of the flesh (senses) and the soul (intellect) are greatly diminished, allowing man's (S)spirit the supremacy that the Bible indicates it so rightly deserves—*and we don't have to die to experience it.* This rule of (S)spirit over the flesh and intellect, which we achieve through meditating, is perpetuated by the renewing of our minds, so that ultimately we "walk in the (S)spirit." Learn to meditate and "hear the music" while you are still alive!

Read the New Testament with your spiritual eyes and ears open and notice how often the expression is used, "He that has an ear (spiritual), let him hear (understand), what the Spirit says to the church." If you sincerely search the Scriptures with your (S)spiritual ears open, you will find the New Testament to be a very *mystical* book, with frequent references to the fourth dimension, or realm of (S)spirit, and its manifestation in the lives of believers. As an aid to you, I have compiled a brief list:

1. The Magi (astrologers) from the East followed the star.
2. Joseph and many others were given spiritual dreams.
3. Peter, James, John, Paul, and Ananias had visions.
4. Peter, James, John, Paul and Ananias heard voices.
5. Paul and companions saw a brilliant light.
6. All apostles witnessed miracles and healings.
7. Angels appeared to several people.
8. Apostles were miraculously set free from prison.
9. Prison door/iron gate opened miraculously for Peter.
10. Earthquake opened prison doors for Paul and Silas.
11. Ananias and Sapphira struck dead in church for lying.
12. Elymas the magician was smitten with blindness.
13. Peter/Paul record being in trances. (Oh, my! *What next?*)
14. Paul had an out-of-the-body experience.
15. Philip was physically translated 25-30 miles to Azotus.
16. Jesus, Peter and Paul raised the dead.
17. Jesus turned water into wine.
18. Jesus multiplied loaves and fishes twice, fed thousands.
19. Jesus walked on water.
20. Jesus frequently manifested supernatural knowledge.
21. Jesus often prophesied of future events.
22. Jesus produced the miraculous draught of fishes.
23. Jesus stilled the storm.
24. Jesus instructed Peter to recover coin in fish's mouth.
25. Jesus disappeared from a crowd on two occasions.

26. Jesus was raised from the dead.
27. Jesus ascended into heaven.
28. Holy Spirit baptism; also speaking with tongues.
29. Gifts of the Holy Spirit given to the church.
30. Demons were cast out.

The list goes on and on but do I need to further impress you with the obvious? The Bible is a *mystical* book, and as such is a handbook of the *supernatural* from cover to cover. Though some would like to do so, *it's too late to change that now!* Yet, the denominational, organizational, natural-minded "mainstream" church has somehow managed to close its eyes to all of this, and has sidestepped the Bible's *mystical* aspects, reducing it to a book of fables, nice stories, moral teachings and nothing more.

Evangelicals go a few steps farther using it as a fire escape from hell and a roadmap to heaven, accepting its teachings for righteous living, but nothing more.

Even many of our Full Gospel, Pentecostal churches which were founded on these great supernatural principles, have laid their torches aside and sold their birthright for a mess of "ecclesiastical pottage." Yet the truth remains that we must accept the Bible for what it is—*the living, active, abiding, supernatural, mystical Word of the Living God.* By so doing we can ensure that the Word will produce the same results today as it did in the First Century—for those who tune in to the realm of (S)spirit! Thus, we can see the urgent need for us to learn *Christian Meditation* in our generation.

East Is East And West Is West

Some time ago, I flew with Dr. Paul Yonggi Cho from Seoul, Korea to Singapore to attend a convocation of world Pentecostal leaders. (Dr. Cho founded, and serves as pastor of a 500,000-member church in Seoul, Korea.) He and I were spending time in deep conversation regarding spiritual things, when I casually asked him, "Do you believe in *Christian Meditation?*" His answer was instantaneous, "O, yes! *Of course I do!*"

Since he had replied so quickly, I was certain he hadn't truly understood my question, so I clarified it: "I don't mean the *Western* concept of meditation where a person simply contemplates a verse of Scripture. I am referring to *Eastern* meditation—quieting oneself in the presence of God, listening for God to speak."

"*Yes, yes!*" Dr. Cho replied excitedly. "That is the *only* way I understand meditation. It is Westerners who have 'Westernized' it to mean something else." He continued, "God gave us *two* ears and only *one* mouth, *so I believe He expects us to listen twice as much as He expects us to speak.*" (O, that *we* would learn that lesson from the Spirit!) Dr. Cho went on to say, "You do not build a great church, as I have, by doing a lot of *talking*—but by doing a lot of *listening* to the voice of the Holy Spirit!"

I am convinced that the church is lacking in its understanding of what prayer is all about. We have reduced it to nothing more than a "spiritual shopping list" (spending all our time telling God what *we* want from *Him*), when prayer is supposed to be a two-way street. There must be a time during prayer in which God has access to the ears of our (S)spirits and can tell us what *He* wants from *us*. (That is, of course, *if* we believe that God still speaks to His children today.) Often, listening may be far, far more important than verbalizing, if it is our true desire to know God's will and direction for our lives.

This concept is rejected out of hand by some, on the grounds that it appears too much like an *Eastern* religion. And well it should—*Christianity was and still is, an Eastern religion!* It is *we* who have Westernized it. For some, an Eastern religion would be one that originated in New Jersey! The church of today will never fully realize either the power or the blessings of God until we return to our Scriptural roots—where the supernatural intervention of God into the affairs of Christians was a natural, accepted and *expected* occurrence in the early Church.

14

INVITED—BUT UNWILLING GUESTS

Meditation is often argued against on the grounds that "gurus, swamis and people of the occult engage in it," which charge smacks to me of "guilt by association." Those same people (occultists) also breathe, eat, sleep and perform a host of other daily functions as well—does that make all *those* things wrong also? Of course not! To argue from such a position is to stand on very thin ice. The pity of all this is that territory which formerly *belonged to the church* has been *relinquished to Satan,* just as Eve yielded her mind to him in Eden. The enemy stepped in quickly to accept that ground and exploit it—and now, because he has laid claim to it, the church fears to *reclaim* it, lest we be associated with the occult. *NONSENSE! IT BELONGS TO US!!* We have allowed him license to it *far* too long already.

And Jesus answered and spoke to them again in parables, saying, "The kingdom of heaven may be compared to a king, who gave a wedding feast for his son. And he sent out his slaves to call those who had been invited to the wedding feast, and they were unwilling to come. Again he sent out other slaves saying, 'Tell those who have been invited, "Behold, I have prepared my dinner; my oxen and my fattened livestock are all butchered and everything is ready; come to the wedding feast."' But they paid no attention and went their way, one to his own farm, another to his business, and the rest seized his slaves and mistreated them and killed them. But the king was enraged and sent his armies, and destroyed those murderers, and set their city on fire. Then he said to his slaves, 'The wedding is ready, but those who were invited were not worthy. Go therefore to the main highways, and as many as you find there, invite to the wedding feast.' And those slaves went out into the streets, and gathered together all they found, both evil and good; and the wedding hall was filled with dinner guests. But when the king came in to look over the dinner guests, he saw there *a man not dressed in wedding clothes,* and he said to him, 'Friend, how did you come in here without wedding clothes?' And he was speechless. Then the king said to servants, 'Bind him hand and foot, and cast him into the outer darkness; in that place there shall be weeping and gnashing of teeth. For many are called, but few are chosen.'" (Matt. 22:1-14; emphasis mine.)

This parable refers explicitly to the *kingdom of heaven*, and not to heaven as a *geographical* location! (Actually, the "kingdom of God" and the "kingdom of heaven" are synonymous, since Jesus used the two terms interchangeably in Matthew 19:23,24. As heaven's kingdom it refers to the *rule* of heaven in that area.) In reading this parable our first discovery is a sad one: "...and he sent out his slaves to call those who had been invited to the wedding feast, and *they were unwilling to come.*" Those who had a *right* by invitation to enter the kingdom were the *very* ones who *rejected* it. I recognize that the primary reference is to the Jews (to whom the kingdom was initially preached); but now since the kingdom has been extended to Gentile believers, it applies to them also, when *they* reject God's kingdom.

An additional reference to this is found in Revelation 3:20:

> Behold, I stand at the door and knock; if anyone hears my voice and opens the door, I will come in to him, and will dine with him, and he with me.

No matter how often you may have heard well-meaning preachers using that verse in impassioned pleas to the unsaved—portraying Jesus as standing at the door of your heart, waiting to come in and save you—it is *not* the intent of that verse! He *is* waiting to come into the hearts of the lost, but that particular verse has absolutely *nothing* to do with the *lost*, and has *everything* to do with the *church!*

In Revelation 1:12,13 Jesus is depicted as the One "...standing in the midst of the seven golden lampstands." The lampstands (which He stood "in the midst of") represent the church. By the third chapter, the church had effectively eased Him out, until He stood *outside* asking to be invited *back in.* That sounds disturbingly similar to the attitudes of so many in our Full Gospel churches today, doesn't it?

Now, back to the parable of the "invited, but unwilling guests." Two invitations were given and rejected, so the invitation was extended to others, who responded favorably. In verse eleven the king came in to greet the wedding guests and found there a man who was not wearing a wedding garment.

The *wedding garment* here is analogous to the garment of the bride of the Lamb in Revelation 19:8:

> And it was granted that she should be arrayed in fine linen, clean and white: *for the fine linen is the righteousness of saints.*

The location of the wedding feast in Matthew's Gospel is the kingdom of heaven, or the kingdom of God. (This is obviously not the geographical *place* called heaven—since *no one* sneaks into heaven *unnoticed*.) It follows then, that if we could discover the location of the kingdom of God, we would then know exactly where this episode took place, and could begin to comprehend the principles being unfolded in this passage. The fact is that we *do* know the exact location of the kingdom—Jesus Himself said, "...for, behold, *the kingdom of God is within you.*" (Luke 17:21; emphasis mine.) The word for "within" is *entos*, which means, "inside; within."

Some Greek scholars have a difficult time translating it "within" when used by Jesus in speaking to the Pharisees, because, as one translator put it, "The Kingdom of God was not in the hearts of the Pharisees." That man may have known a lot about the Greek, but he obviously knew little about the kingdom of God.

The domain (or kingdom) of God, Who is Spirit, has always been *man's spirit*. Before we go on, let me define "spirit" for you according to the Greek:

> *Pneuma:* Current of air, i.e. breath, blast, breeze—a spirit i.e. (human) the rational soul, (by implication) vital principle, mental disposition, etc.: or (superhuman) angel, demon or (divine) God, Christ's spirit, the Holy Spirit—ghost, life, spirit (ual, ually), mind.

It is clear that all humans have spirits—and that their spirits are a part of God, Who is Spirit—even though they are separated (called "spiritual death") from Him. Their spirits are *still* His kingdom, although He may not *reign* there due to a lack of invitation. We have previously seen that man was created *primarily* as a spirit-being who *secondarily* possessed a soul and who *incidently* lived in a body.

It could be argued that a kingdom must have a king actively ruling and reigning over it. But that is not necessarily the case, as has been demonstrated numerous times throughout history. Rightful kings, for one reason or another, have been deposed and have left their kingdoms with the hope of returning. Such a ruler becomes a king in exile. His absence does not abolish the kingdom, but only temporarily limits his right to rule therein. That sounds very much like the King of Revelation Chapter 3—*exiled* and standing outside, requesting permission to come in. This was also the case when Jesus spoke concerning the kingdom of God being within the Pharisees. In essence, Jesus was saying, "You

Pharisees are looking for the kingdom of God and don't even realize that it is right under your spiritual noses—it is within you! God's domain is not a physical, earthly kingdom, it is your *spirits.*"

The kingdom is in man's spirit because it is a *spiritual* kingdom, or kingdom of spirit. Aren't you, as a Christian, part of His kingdom? Of course you are! Does He *reign as absolute sovereign and Lord* in your (S)spirit and life? Probably not! We are too often willing to accept Him as *Savior,* yet ignore Him as *Lord!* We thus establish a kingdom without a reigning king (Lord, absolute sovereign)!

Now that you understand the location of the kingdom of God, let us return to our parable of the "invited, but unwilling guests." We discovered that there was a man attending the feast (inside the kingdom/spirit), even though he was improperly attired (not having on a wedding garment/righteousness). Since our (S)spirits are a part of God, there is awesome power resident within us; and though the unsaved have no right to enter—they often do. Believers, who have a divine birthright to enter and see (be aware of) the kingdom within, most often do not.

Matthew 13:24-30; 36-43 contributes strong evidence to the fact that those who are not Christians have access to the kingdom of God!

> Then He left the multitudes and went into the house. And His disciples came to Him, saying. "Explain to us the parable of the tares of the field." And He answered and said, "the one who sows the good seed is the Son of Man, and the field is the world; and as for the good seed, these are the sons of the kingdom; and the tares are the sons of the evil one; and the enemy who sowed them is the devil, and the harvest is the end of the age; and the reapers are angels. Therefore just as the tares are gathered up and burned with fire, so shall it be at the end of the age. The Son of Man will send forth His angels, and they will *gather out of His kingdom* all stumbling blocks, and *those who commit lawlessness* and will cast them into the furnace of fire; in that place there shall be weeping and gnashing of teeth. Then the righteous will shine forth as the sun in the kingdom of their Father. He who has ears, let him hear. (Verses 36-43; emphasis mine.)

Verse forty-one states that, "The Son of Man will send forth His angels, and they will *gather out of His kingdom* all stumbling blocks, and *those who commit lawlessness.*" The gathering is "out of His kingdom," confirming the premise that those who do not belong in His kingdom, *still have access to it*—and that access will continue until "...the end of the age...." The Bible says that those who are gathered out will be, "all stumbling blocks, and *those who commit lawlessness*." These are two very interesting terms in the Greek. Stumbling block also means "offend"; and there are at least two ways in which their trespass has caused offense: 1. Their presence in the kingdom is a definite offense to God. 2. They are offensive to immature Christians who stumble when they see supernatural acts (similar to those wrought by the Holy Spirit) being performed by those involved with the occult. They then stumble further when, because they fear contamination with the occult, they "throw the baby out with the bath-water" and reject the genuine works of the Holy Spirit.

Why are these trespassers an offense to God and Christians? Because they are "those who commit lawlessness," although this isn't the clearest rendition from the Greek to English. It is better translated as, "those who are in violation of law!" What law are they in violation of? It certainly does not refer to the Jewish (Mosiac) Law, since as Christians we are not under the law, as Galatians 3:11 says so eloquently:

> Now that *no one is justified by the Law* before God is evident; for "The righteous man shall live by faith." (Emphasis mine.)

Jesus also said:

> Truly, truly, I say to you, he who does not enter by the door, into the fold of the sheep, *but climbs up some other way,* he is a thief, and a robber. (Jn. 10:1; emphasis mine.)

Jesus further said:

> I am the door; if anyone enters through Me, he shall be saved, and shall go *in and out,* and find pasture. (Jn. 10:9; emphasis mine.)

Here then, is where those who are an offense to God are "in violation of law"—*they are coming by some other way than the ONE way provided by God Himself!*

Lastly, we have yet another Scriptural insight into the fact that others who are not born of God do have access, though not legally, to the kingdom of God:

> The kingdom of heaven is like a mustard seed, which a man took and sowed in his field; and this is smaller than all the other seeds; but when it is full grown, it is larger than the garden plants, and becomes a tree, *so that the birds of the air* (heavens, ed.) *come and nest in its branches.* (Matt. 13:31, 32; emphasis mine.)

Many Bible scholars believe that the reference to birds here has to do with demonic spirits, as in Matthew 13:4,19, "...and as he sowed, some seeds fell beside the road, and the birds came and devoured them." Jesus stated, in explaining this parable:

> ...When anyone hears *THE WORD OF THE KINGDOM,* and does not understand it, *THE EVIL ONE* (Satan, ed.) comes and snatches away what has been sown in his heart (mind, ed.). This is the one on whom seed was sown beside the road. (Emphasis mine.)

Jesus thus established that His figurative use of birds was analogous to demonic spirits whose primary purpose is to keep Christians from discovering the truth which would set them free. So, those birds of the heavens actually *nest* in the branches—*make their abode* in the kingdom of heaven!

Take particular notice of the sequence of events in the aforementioned parable:

> When anyone hears the word of the kingdom, and does not understand it, *(then,* ed.) the evil one (Satan, ed.) comes and snatches away what has been sown in his heart (mind, ed.)

Jesus taught very clearly—and emphaticly—that *UNDERSTANDING THE WORD OF THE KINGDOM* is what prevents the devil from stealing the Word of God out of our minds. What, then, is "the word of the kingdom"? It would take volumes to do justice to that question, but I will attempt to distill the gist of it into a few sentences. Briefly, the message (or word) of the kingdom is that *Jesus Christ is Lord!* As such, He is absolute Sovereign, and has established His kingdom in the hearts of believers, through whom He manifests His power over all the works of the devil. That is how Jesus said we would recognize that the kingdom had arrived—Satan and all his evil cohorts, along with their nefarious deeds, would fall beneath the onslaughts of the Church of Jesus Christ! "And the God of peace will soon crush Satan *under your feet."* (Rom.

16:20; emphasis mine.) In Luke 11:20 Jesus said, "But if I cast out demons by the finger of God, *THEN THE KINGDOM OF GOD HAS COME UPON YOU,*" establishing *this* as a sign of the kingdom of God—*that demons, and therefore all their evil works,* would be subject to the authority of the Christ Spirit within us.

Now, let us return to the parable of the birds (evil spirits) who nest (make their abode in) the kingdom of God. We have already recognized that the kingdom of God is the *spirit* of every person born into the world, even though Christ may not be presently reigning there. I realize that this concept may seem foreign to some, but we must recognize that we are dealing with the realm of *spirit,* and all of these forces, whether good or evil, are all of the same "stuff." As we discovered earlier in this chapter, the English translation of the all-inclusive word *pneuma,* from which we derive the word "spirit" denotes *all* categories of "spirit." Therefore, it should not seem foreign to us that unregenerate man is capable of entering the realm or dimension of his spirit, since spirit seems to have access to all other realms of spirit. This is continually being demonstrated by the unsaved employing such means as E.S.P., spiritism, hypnosis, transcendental meditation, and other occult practices too numerous to mention here. These people have *ABSOLUTELY NO LEGAL RIGHT TO BE IN THE KINGDOM!* But they *are* there—while born-again believers (who not only have the prerogative to enter this domain, but who possess a *divine birthright* and *mandate* to enter it), mostly stay on the outside. Often they refuse to enter because of fear—fear of the unknown, usually caused by a lack of information. For years they have attended churches which not only do not believe in the supernatural, but who ardently fight it and forbid their followers to have anything to do with it. The days of spiritual ignorance are fast coming to a close, as the Church awakens to its rights and privileges to function in the (S)spirit realm. It is my hope that this book and my seminars will play some small part in helping to open the door of the fourth dimension to sincere believers who fervently desire to claim their spiritual heritage.

15

TRANCES

Entering into the (S)spirit is to initiate contact with the fourth dimension—something each believer is called upon to experience. Man's soul (mind) is a bridge between his (S)spirit and his *body*; therefore we should expect certain mental and/or physiological changes to occur upon encountering the realm of (S)spiritual experience. Since we admittedly know so little about this subject, the following information should not be construed as being in any way complete and absolute. It is simply an *introduction*—a mere opening of the door we seek to enter. In future years scientific research will probably add far more comprehensive material to the rudimentary knowledge we possess on this subject today.

And on the next day, as they were on their way, and approaching the city, Peter went up on the housetop about the sixth hour (noon, ed.) to pray. And he became hungry, and was desiring to eat; but while they were making preparations; *he fell into a trance.* (Acts 10:9,10; emphasis mine.)

Peter, during his explanation of that experience to the council at Jerusalem, said:

I was in the city of Joppa praying; and *in a trance* I saw a vision.... (Acts 11:5; emphasis mine.)

It should be noted here that, while Peter felt constrained to offer a statement to the Jerusalem council concerning why he had fellowship with ceremonially unclean Gentiles, *not a single word was offered in defense of having been "in a trance."* Rather, the trance and what transpired during it were offered as Peter's *rationale* for his actions. It would seem that an occurrence such as this was considered by the early Church fathers to be a valid and acceptable experience!

Notice the similarity of Paul's experience in Acts 22:17,18a where, once again, absolutely no defense is tendered for having been "in a trance":

And it came about when I returned to Jerusalem and was praying in the temple, that *I fell into a trance,* and I saw Him saying to me.... (Emphasis mine.)

The foregoing are three of the most ignored portions in the entire Bible. I have the distinct impression that some people feel if they disregard these verses consistently they will simply go away, but since they are inspired Scripture, we cannot afford to overlook them! However, since occultists have so often trespassed in this area, the Church has been reluctant to consider the existence of trances as a legitimate part of the Christian experience. Yet the early Church obviously did so.

When forced to confront the fact that trances are mentioned in the New Testament (something they are loathe to do), trance opponents attempt to sidestep the issue by saying that "trance" really doesn't mean "trance" in the *mystical* sense, as we imply; but simply means "a heightened state of awareness" or something else entirely different (although they aren't sure *exactly* what). That argument is about as weak as the broth made from the shadow of a chicken that starved to death!!

The Greek is *most explicit* leaving absolutely no doubt of Peter and Paul's meaning. The word is *ekstasis*, which means *"a displacement of the mind* i.e. bewilderment, ecstasy, to be amazed, trance, to put (stand) out of wits, become astounded, insane, be beside self, bewitch, wonder." This definition is impossible to argue with since it even links this state of mind to insanity—in the sense that the mind of someone in a trance is not his own. For that brief moment in time, his mind belongs to the Holy Spirit.

One of the definitions is "to be beside self," which is a good description of what sometimes transpires during a trance. During some visions, (which often occur during the trance state), one has the distinct impression of standing out of the body, while viewing some panorama in the realm of (S)spirit. Many of the visions recorded in Scripture seem to intimate that this was the experience of the prophet of record. Consider the words of the Apostle Paul as he relates one such experience:

> Boasting is necessary, though it is not profitable; but I will go on to visions and revelations of the Lord. I know a man in Christ who fourteen years ago—*whether in the body I do not know, or out of the body I do not know,* God knows— such a man was caught up to the third heaven. And I know how such a man was—*whether in the body or apart from the body I do not know,* God knows—was caught up into paradise and heard inexpressible words, which a man is not permitted to speak. (II Cor. 12:1-4, emphasis mine.)

I can remember a similar incident from my own experience, in which I was so enraptured by the presence of the Holy Spirit that I was transported out of my body: I was preaching the Word and had become so totally yielded to the Holy Spirit that I suddenly found myself standing outside my body, several feet away and off to one side. For the remainder of my sermon, I was simply a bystander, observing the Holy Spirit in absolute control of my body. It wasn't at all frightening—but I was absolutely "beside myself" (no pun intended) with amazement!

W.E. Vine defines "trance" from the Greek, thusly:

> Denotes a trance, a condition in which *ordinary consciousness* and the perception of natural circumstances were *withheld,* and the soul (mind) was susceptible *only to the vision imparted by God,* or again, a condition in which a person is so *transported out of his natural state* that he falls into a trance. (Emphasis mine.)

It would seem from this definition, and my own and others' experiences, that this is the most absolute form of yieldedness to the Holy Spirit. My, how the natural man struggles to retain his *own* control over his mind and thought processes, and tends to fear everything which threatens his concept of "stability." Anything impinging upon that balance of *self*-control is frightening because, whether consciously or subconsciously, this is how we measure "sanity." Yet Paul said, "If we are beside ourselves (insane, ed.) it is to God...." (II Cor. 5:13)

One of the major arguments put forth by trance opponents is that, "We should never lose control of our ability to be *in* control." My first question to them, of course, would be, "What Scripture proof-text is that decision based upon?" Secondly, "What is so glorious about denying the Holy Spirit *His* right to absolute control over our minds?" Thirdly, "Why should we believe that *our* minds can safeguard us better than the mind of Christ?" Fourthly, "How did you arrive at the mistaken notion that our minds have *no* control whatsoever during a trance state?" We will return to these questions shortly, and analyze them in greater depth.

In the narrative found in John 11:1-13 Jesus was instructing His disciples concerning certain principles of prayer:

> Now suppose one of you fathers is asked by his son for a fish; he will not give him a snake instead of a fish, will he? Or if he is asked for an egg, he will not give him a scorpion, will he? If you then, be-

ing evil, know how to give good gifts to your children, *how much more* shall your heavenly Father give the Holy Spirit to those who ask Him. (Verses 11-13; emphasis mine.)

Jesus thus illustrated that even wicked people respond in love to their children's requests, and would never expose them to anything harmful such as scorpions and snakes (which are *always* synonymous with *demons*). When entering into meditation, the Christian's only goal is to have an encounter with the Holy Spirit within. It is simply inconceivable that a loving heavenly Father would permit evil spirits to respond to our desire for more of Him! Paul said, "...for I know whom I have believed and I am convinced that *He is able to guard what I have entrusted to Him* until that day." (I Tim. 1:12; emphasis mine.) I am likewise persuaded!

When I meditate, I entrust my (S)spirit and mind to the Holy Spirit and am fully convinced of His ability (and willingness) to guard what I have entrusted to Him. If we *can't* trust Him, where can we find a God whom we *can* trust? When meditating I do not consider it possible that some uninvited, undesired, evil spirit (which has no part with me) could invade my (S)spirit (which belongs to God). I have *committed* my (S)spirit to God—and it is His 24 hours out of every day—*even when I meditate!*

It was said of the prophet Balaam:

> ...Balaam the son of Beor...the man whose eyes are opened...which heard the words of God, which saw the vision of the Almighty, *falling into a trance, but having his eyes open.* (Num. 24:3,4; K.J.V.; emphasis mine.)

It should be noted here that while Balaam is most remembered as a potential "prophet for hire," the above description was given when "the Spirit of God came upon him." (vs.2)

Of King Saul we read:

> ...and the spirit of God came upon him also, so that he went along prophesying continually until he came to Naioth in Ramah. And he also stripped off his clothes, and he too prophesied before Samuel and lay down naked all that day and all that night.... (I Sam. 19:23,24; emphasis mine.)

I mention these two narratives only to illustrate that sometimes the Spirit of God moves in other than a humanly anticipated *or humanly acceptable* manner! Both Balaam and Saul experienced trances—Balaam with his eyes open (which is the deepest form of trance). Occasionally when meditating, the trance state will occur, always accompanied by a profound sense of the presence of the Holy Spirit, which lingers long after the trance has lifted. It is never, I repeat, *never* something to be feared. I warmly anticipate such intimacy of (S)spirit when meditating, since I come away knowing my (S)spirit and the Holy Spirit have been in uninterrupted fellowship and that *He*, not *I*, has been in control. How refreshingly welcome!

ALTERED STATES

Basically, a trance (by Scriptural definition) is "an altered state of consciousness." Altered simply means "changed; different"—not "evil"! Trances are altered states of consciousness, not *un*consciousness since, during a trance, our consciousness is directed inward (where the Holy Spirit dwells). Even though the outer (conscious) mind is inactive, the inner (subconscious) mind is continually alert and aware of what is transpiring around and within us. This has been amply illustrated in medical journals where accounts have been given of patients having heard conversations among the operating room staff even while under heavy sedation. Everyone who has ever undergone general anesthesia has been in an "altered state of consciousness" and so has anyone who has ever *daydreamed, taken an aspirin or gone to sleep at night!*

While anesthetized or asleep, *with your conscious mind totally suspended,* who has been "in control" of you then? Aside from the thought which some express that altered states of consciousness, (which *sleep* is) may open you to demonic influence—aren't you simply afraid that you will fall out of bed? Why not? Could it be because you know that there is a part of you functioning at the subconscious level that never sleeps and is watching over you twenty-four hours a day? Allow me to illustrate:

A new mother arrives home from the hospital, exhausted from her nine-month-long ordeal and delivery. Wearily she goes to bed and sleeps the deep sleep that only a new mother can appreciate. (My wife, the mother of five, has told me of this.) A nearby explosion would probably not disturb her rest—but let that precious newborn simply whimper and she is on her feet in a moment! There is a subconscious part of her that is aware of her surroundings, sorts out the irrelevant from the relevant and only allows her to be roused if the situation warrants it.

If you can trust that part of you while you sleep, or while you are anesthetized, why should it be so difficult to apply that *same trust* while meditating?

The Real Fear

What many actually mean when they speak of their "fear of losing control" is rather that they fear losing *conscious* control. Somehow we have mistakenly placed a premium upon our conscious minds that cannot be validated by Scripture—or by science. The conscious mind has a rather limited scope of 7+ or -2 bits of information that it can successfully attend to at any one moment. About thirty years ago George Miller reported the results of his human and animal perceptual research in his paper *"The Magic Number 7+ or -2."* He had discovered that humans have the capacity to handle approximately seven pieces of information at the conscious level at any one time, and when that number is exceeded a person experiences "overload" and begins to make mistakes.

Conversely, the subconscious arena seems to have an *absolutely unlimited capacity.* Dr. David Samuels of the Weizmann Institute estimates that during every minute of our lives the brain is engaged in carrying out between 100,000 and 1,000,000 chemical reactions. The average brain has more than 10,000,000,000 (ten billion) neurons or nerve cells with interconnections (or degrees of freedom) that are so enormous it would require a line of digits the size of the type in this book, stretched over 6,000,000 miles to record it. This means that at any given moment *the subconscious has hundreds of millions of options at its disposal*—slightly more than the conscious mind's 7+ or -2. Wouldn't you agree? We attempt (usually futilely) to affect change at the subconscious level (with its hundreds of millions of options) by using the conscious mind with its severely limited 7+ or -2 options *and then wonder why we have lost the battle.* Following this course of action is comparable to resisting an atom bomb with a firecracker—yet we persist in it most of our lives! WHY?

CAN WE TALK?

In Ephesians 4:23,24 we are admonished to *"...be renewed in the spirit of your mind,* and *put on* the *new self...."* (Emphasis mine.) Please read Romans 12:1,2; the fourth chapter of Ephesians; and the entire book of Colossians (especially Col.3:10) with its many references to the fact that it is *our* responsibility to affect change in our minds (which will ultimately change our actions). The Bible is replete with references which clearly indicate that once saved, it is *we* who must renew our minds.

Since God has exhorted *us* to renew our minds, it would be most unfair if He had not provided some effective means by which that goal could be accomplished. He has indeed furnished a way to reach the subconscious and affect necessary change but, for the most part, ecclesiasticals know little or nothing about it. Some condemn out-of-hand that about which they know nothing. When a Christian approaches the pastor or other spiritual leader and exposes some area of weakness with which they struggle, what hope for permanent change is extended to them? Sometimes they are confronted with psychological jargon and at best come away understanding *why* they act as they do. But people don't necessarily want to know *why* they conduct themselves in a certain fashion—they want to be instructed in *how* to *change* their behavior. The preponderance of counselling normally consists of Christian catch-phrases which freely translate into: "Read your Bible and pray." Or "You could change if you really wanted to!" If this were all the direction needed, then the Bible would have only one line of instruction for Christian behavior. It would have simply said, "Read your Bible and pray"—but it says *far* more than that! Please don't misunderstand me—we *must* pray and read the Bible faithfully. I live in the Word of God and pray hours every day, but as I have discovered, these essential exercises *by themselves* may *not* affect the needed change for many people.

During the first *10%* of our lives we are programmed with neural patterns (linkages of brain cells which determine habits, etc.) that will influence how we will live during the remaining *90%*. In other words, what we have "learned"(?) in the first 7-8 years of life will govern our responses (therefore, what we *become*) over the course of the remaining 62-72 years. This doesn't even include bad habits and thought patterns that we will develop later in life, which will *also* have to be dealt with if we are to live in victory and with renewed minds. But how does one "get at" these "nasty neurons" in order to change them?

D.O.S. — BOSS — S.O.S.

These neural patterns are, for the most part, in the domain of our subconscious and do *not* respond very well (and often *not at all*) to conscious efforts to change them. When you analyze it, that really does explain a great deal. For instance, how often have you started a diet on *Monday*—only to crash in defeat by *Wednesday?*

Or perhaps being overweight is not your problem, but a *dirty mind* is. How often have you struggled within yourself saying, "I won't *ever* think another thought like that again"—only to have it grip you *the very next time* a similar stimulus was present?

Your own individual problem may be one of a thousand others that lack of space prevents me from mentioning—but *you* know what it is. *You know only too well what it is,* because you struggle with it every day of your life! You have diligently exerted *conscious* effort in a futile attempt to modify your behavior, and time after time many of you have given up. I can just hear the familiar refrain: "Why try?...Why bother to expend the energy when nothing works?...I'm sick and tired of being defeated by this problem, but what can I do?" Plaintive cries, all of them—*but there is hope!*

As I have mentioned previously, I am writing this book on a computer. Said computer has an "operating system" which is reffered to as D.O.S. (for *D*isk *O*perating *S*ystem). It is the "brains" behind all that this computer is capable of doing and my computer will not function without it. So that makes D.O.S the BOSS! If there is something in a program that I don't like I use "D.O.S the BOSS" to change it. The subconscious mind is analogous to D.O.S. in that it is the BOSS, and if you are going to change you will have to learn how to use it. Your subconscious mind is *not* your enemy—aside from God it is your best friend. It sets up certain reactions and habit patterns to protect you or to facilitate matters because it assumes (rightly or wrongly) that you want it done that way. When it behaves negatively it does so because it operates very much like a computer: *GIGO—G*arbage *I*n, *G*arbage *O*ut! *In order to reprogram it you must gain access to it*—and *that*, in large part, is what *Christian Meditation* is all about—instructing you how to gain access to your inner self.

Since my earliest recollections I struggled my entire life with an intense fear of rejection that *no* amount of religious exercise was able to overcome. Then the Holy Spirit began to reveal how I could renew my mind in this area using techniques of *Christian Meditation* with which I was already familiar. *Christian Meditation* allows us to bypass the conscious mind and enter the realm of the *subconscious* where change can be most easily accomplished. The results were not only encouraging, but staggering. *In ten minutes' time a persistent personality trait that had plagued me for forty-eight years had vanished without a trace.* Be assured that this is not an *isolated* instance in my experience—I have also successfully altered *several* other habit patterns in my life, which had for many years succeeded in resisting change through the use of my conscious mind alone.

It is close to impossible to alter the subconscious mind by *conscious* effort alone, and we prove this by our consistently high failure rate. Most Christians have no argument with those who *consciously* attempt to revamp their behavior, but become *most* vociferous when any mention is made of using the *subconscious* mind for the same purpose. Doesn't it seem strange that there is little or no resistance to the use of that which has almost *no* influence to affect change—the conscious mind? Conversely, there is *much* clamor over the utilization of the single most powerful tool for change that God has given us—our subconscious minds! What force do you suppose is behind that? The answer might become obvious if you ask yourself, "Who has the most to gain by my continued defeat?"

USE THE RIGHT TOOL, FOOL!

When I was just a young boy I attended shop class. You know the kind of class—the one where you learn to make a pump-handle lamp and other "utilitarian" things like that. Some wood had to be removed and a chisel was required for the job. None was at hand, so I improvised—I used a screwdriver. After all, they do look somewhat alike, and even though it took more effort to use the wrong tool, I *was* getting *some* results, albeit *sloppy* ones. Then a voice spoke from behind me (one that was altogether too familiar—the voice of my shop teacher, Mr. Lynch), "Use the right tool, fool!"

He was right! One of the earliest lessons he had taught us was that you never, *ever* use a tool for *any* purpose other than the one for which is was intended. To do so was not only foolhardy, but *dangerous*. Yet many Christians (including ecclesiastical leaders) are similarly guilty of misusing the "tools" that God has placed at our disposal by insisting that the *conscious* mind is the *only* proper tool to utilize when attempting to modify habit patterns which are resident in the *subconscious*. Having established repeatedly that this route nearly always leads to abject failure, they blindly pursue it anyway. The rationale seems to be: "We don't have to have a *reason* for what we do. It's just the way we've *always* done it." That reminds me of a story:

> It was a holiday and the entire family had gathered to celebrate. As mother was preparing the festive ham, she cut one end off. Her daughter asked her why she did that, and mother answered that *her* mother had always cut the end off. So daughter went to grandma and asked her why *she* had always cut off the end of the ham. To which she replied, "Because *my* mother always cut the end of the ham off." So daughter went to great grandma and asked her why *she* always cut the end of the ham off, to which the simple answer was, "Because my roasting pan was too small!" What creatures of habit we are!

ONE FINAL THOUGHT

Few would argue the fact that the ability to enter into an altered state of consciousness (daydreaming, sleep,etc.) is an *innate* operation of the mind. Thus it is really no different from any other normal bodily function. Since this faculty is resident in man as an *inborn* ability, we must rightly conclude that it was created by *God* and therefore serves some God-given purpose. It has been branded as "evil" by *many* because it is understood by *so few*. I understand the many misuses and abuses by those in the world (see chapter 14), but that should not serve as justification for Christians to write this subject off and sweep it under some ecclesiastical rug as though it did not exist.

Other bodily capacities and functions are *grossly* abused also, *often within the Church!* Yet the legitimate, God-given function *itself* is not decried from the pulpit.

Without a healthy appetite for food we would soon die, but through *misuse* of food we see large numbers of *inordinately obese people* in the church. Though this is a fact, when was the last time you heard a sermon or read a book lamenting the universal practice of *eating*?

The sex drive is also a normal physical appetite given to man by God during creation, when He instructed him to "...be fruitful and multiply, and fill the earth...." (Gen.1:28). No one would debate that sex is sometimes abused and misused by people in the church, yet you have probably never heard a sermon or read a book against sex itself!

The thirst for learning is yet another drive that originates with God, nevertheless relationships have been destroyed by those who carried their quest for knowledge to ridiculous extremes. Have you ever heard a sermon or read a book attacking education?

To continue illustrating this point would only serve redundancy. However, when confronted with the *equally God-given faculty* of *Christian Meditation* which allows us to enter into altered states of consciousness, how do the church leaders deal with the subject? Well, since it's not as much fun as eating or engaging in sex or reading, and since most of them know nothing about the subject, *they preach sermons against it and write books assaulting it*. Instead, they should decry only the *abuses* and leave the way clear for Christians to meditate, using the subconscious mind for the renewing of the mind and hearing the voice of God. Sadly, mankind has *always* attacked what it has not understood—*that is the nature of man!*

16

MEDIUMS AND TRANCES

One of the major arguments opponents use against trances is that spiritist mediums engage in them and allow evil spirits (demons), to assume control over their minds, personalities and voices. This is true. However, as we have already established, the criteria for or against anything is not, and never has been whether occultists engage in it, but rather what the Bible has to say on the subject.

For instance, some spiritists speak in tongues but I am not about to relinquish my Scriptural right and privilege to talk in tongues and edify my (S)spirit. I have also seen spiritists practice the laying on of hands, and praying for the sick—but I refuse to yield even one word of Jesus' promise, "They shall lay hands on the sick and they shall recover." I have seen spiritists reveal with accuracy the thoughts of those in their audience—but I still hold dear to me the Scriptural gift of the word of knowledge through which I have ministered to thousands over the years, revealing the thoughts of their hearts and the sicknesses in their bodies! Spiritists quote the Bible, but that does not diminish its standing as the written Word of God.

The above perversions of sacred things are simply examples of Satanic counterfeiting! The Word of God is replete with illustrations where Satan attempted to duplicate the works of God. (See Ex. 7:8-12; 20-22; 8:6,7.) He is busily engaged in the same nonsense today; but we must beware lest *we destroy (or refuse) the genuine in order to avoid the counterfeit.*

We recently experienced a rash of counterfeit ten dollar bills here in Chicago. The fact is that this "bogus business" came rather close to home when my son found two of them in his wallet. Our immediate reaction was to invite our friends together, gather all our ten dollar bills into a pile and burn them, thus by burning them all, we would certainly destroy any "funny money" also. Absurd? Of course it is! No one in his right mind would even consider destroying the genuine in order to root out the counterfeit—that's insanity at its zenith! (This truth is borne out in Jesus' parable of the wheat and tares—see Matthew 13:24-30.) Of course, we were genuinely concerned that we not be taken in by the counterfeits that were making the rounds in our city; but we allowed our concern to take the form of *caution*, looking *very carefully* at all ten dollar bills before accepting them.

If I had destroyed all my ten dollar bills, you would say (and rightly so) that I was certifiably insane. Yet few question the mentality and/or the motivation of *doctrinal* "ten dollar bill burners," who routinely dismiss as evil *any and all* mystical practices on the grounds that "occultists and spiritists engage in similar activities—therefore it's *all* counterfeit!" Actually, the presence of a counterfeit is a testimonial to the existence of a genuine.

You cannot rule out anything spiritual on the grounds that "occultists and spiritists do it." That is absolutely unacceptable theological practice—and anyone who argues from that point is NO THEOLOGIAN! To use such reasoning in college would be to fail Basic Theology; and anyone engaging in such nonsense while claiming theological expertise, does the Word of God and his students a genuine disservice! The Bible, *God's Word,* is the *final* and *absolute* yardstick by which we measure all truth or error!! We will come back to this premise in a later chapter.

Before we progress, I must go on record here as stating that I agree totally with God's Word which is *diametrically opposed to the premise of spiritism and communicating with the "dead" (demons).* The Word of God is *most* explicit in its objections to, and prohibitions of, this practice—*that is not debatable!* (See Lev. 20:6,27; Deut. 18:9-12.) However I do wish to examine mediumship and the resultant trances that occur, only because there are spiritual principles involved which they have prostituted to their own evil purposes. If they have counterfeited them, we need to be aware of and covet earnestly the genuine.

When a spiritist enters into a trance he/she becomes a medium, a *bridge* linking humans with the spirit (demonic) realm. The medium hears the voices of spirits (demons), sees things in the spirit realm and relates what is heard and/or seen to the congregation. Some mediums yield themselves so totally to the "controlling spirit guide" (demon), that their voices change and the spirit (demon) actually speaks through them. They are entering the lower end of the realm of spirit, not having been born of the Holy Spirit. (If they are so eager to yield to the influence of unholy (demonic) forces, why are Christians so reluctant to yield themselves to the absolute control of the Holy Spirit?)

Conversely it was said of Jesus, "He whom God has sent *speaks the words of God.*" (Jn. 3:34a; emphasis mine.)

And again:

> But He (Jesus) answered them, "My Father is working until now, and I Myself am working..." Jesus therefore answered and was saying to them, "Truly, truly, I say to you, the Son can do nothing of Himself, *unless it is something He sees the Father doing*; for whatever the Father does, these things the Son also does in like

manner. For the Father loves the Son, *and shows Him all things that He Himself is doing*; and greater works than these will He show Him, that you may marvel...I can do nothing on my own initiative. As I hear I judge....'' (Jn. 5:17,19,20,30; emphasis mine.)

Jesus' ministry was limited, according to His own admission, to doing only those things He *SAW* the Father doing. Obviously, Jesus lived in the realm of Spirit and revelation knowledge, and was *constantly* aware of the Father's movement and activity; therefore, His *every* action and His *every* word was in direct harmony with the will of God. Even a cursory examination of the life and ministry of Jesus should be enough to convince anyone that there was a definite correlation between His ongoing insight into the realm of Spirit and the powerful ministry that followed.

In Galatians 5:16 we are enjoined to ''...walk in the Spirit....'' and in subsequent verses the Apostle Paul described the battle of the flesh versus the (S)spirit. In this passage of Scripture, the translators capitalized the word ''spirit,'' indicating Holy Spirit. However, since the Greek word for ''spirit'' is not specific unless preceded by the word ''Holy'' or ''God's,'' or followed by the words ''of God'' or ''of Jesus,'' we may rightly conclude that the reference here is to *man's* spirit. As Scripture verifies, there really is no difference between God's Spirit and mans *born again (S)spirit:* ''But the one who joins himself to the Lord is *one spirit* with Him.'' (I Cor. 6:17; emphasis mine.) So, when we enter our (S)spirits, which have been born from above, we are venturing into the kingdom of God and have become *one* with the Holy Spirit.

Since a lack of space here precludes my quoting the entire eighth chapter of Romans, may I exhort you to read it—many times. It is one of the finest Biblical expositions on the Holy Spirit and His all-important role in our lives. I will quote only key portions here:

> For all who are being led by the Spirit of God, *these* are the sons of God...and in the same way the Spirit also helps our weakness; for we do not know how to pray as we should, *but the Spirit Himself intercedes for us* with groanings too deep for words; and He who searches the hearts knows what the mind of the Spirit is, because He intercedes for the saints according to the will of God. (Verses 14,26,27; emphasis mine.)

The word for ''weakness'' is translatable as ''feebleness of body or mind.'' The Spirit knows what our minds cannot comprehend—that which is our deepest and most urgent need and He prays accordingly, in full compliance with the will of God!

There is no way to adequately stress the extreme importance of knowing the will of God in any given circumstance; yet many Christians have absolutely no knowledge of how to enter the realm of (S)spirit to ascertain it. Others suppress their born again (S)spirit when it attempts to assert its rightful position of authority. I believe this is the reason why Paul wrote in I Thessalonians 5:19, "Quench not the spirit." Simply put, quench means "to extinguish," as one might snuff out a flame.

It was said of Watchman Nee, the great Chinese Christian author, that he had an advanced gift of the "word of knowledge," and received many revelations; but because he felt they were from his soul and not from God, he fought his (S)spirit and successfully quenched/extinguished its activities. Who knows how very much greater and far-reaching his ministry might have been had he opened himself to the realm of the (S)spirit? May we never be found quilty of quenching the (S)spirit in our lives!

17

LEARNING TO HEAR THE VOICE OF GOD

For some gifted Christians, hearing the voice of God comes easily—without any apparent effort; while other, equally sincere Christians go through life in a spiritual vacuum. Yet we are told that "...God is no respecter of persons." How then do we equate the *apparent* disparity between the spiritual experiences (or lack of them) of these two groups? Are we to conclude that there are some "favored few" who have access, not only to God's ear, but also to His voice? I think not. Admittedly, there *are* some people who (whether by temperament, personality, or some unknown inner faculty) experience greater ease of entrance into the dimension of (S)spirit. But the fact that some enter more easily than others should by no means exclude the countless numbers of others who struggle, yearning deeply to know God's voice! They simply need more help to do so. I believe it is part of the spiritual heritage of all Christians to walk in the fourth dimension of (S)spirit.

In the Old Testament, the Books of the Kings tell of the great prophet Samuel who was accompanied by "sons of the prophets" at Ramah, which appears to be a place of apprenticeship and learning. This group is often referred to by Biblical scholars as "The School of The Prophets," because of their student-teacher relationship with the prophet, Samuel.

A similar situation is repeated in II Kings, chapter six, where the prophet Elisha was surrounded by "sons of the prophets." The place where they dwelled became too small for their number (indicating that they were taking in new students), so they engaged in a building program to accommodate their expansion. Again, we find a "School of The Prophets." I am convinced that these schools were *not* theological seminaries as we understand them, since there is absolutely no evidence that these young men were being prepared as Levites or teachers—*they were being trained to become prophets.* Therefore, I am persuaded these were "schools" where men whose (S)spirits were open could learn how to become sensitive to the Holy Spirit and hear God's voice!

Just as there are many voices and pictures in the atmosphere surrounding us and we fail to see or hear them without the proper equipment, even so the voice of God is ever speaking to His Church and we often fail to hear or see into that dimension for lack of training! Yet there *are* things we could do (if we knew what they were) to enable us to enter the realm of (S)spirit, things which help us tune out the *physical* world about us, and tune in to the Holy Spirit.

As I said earlier, there are some who stumble on these things quite by accident and *I* am among that company of people. Allow me to explain. Years ago, on the evangelistic field, I developed the practice of consistantly praying six to eight hours daily before ministering to long lines of the sick nightly. Toward the end of my prayer marathons, lying wearily and nearly asleep across my bed, I would find myself drifting into the realm between waking and sleeping—and in *that* state I would often experience supernatural visitations. Frequently I saw visions of future events (often what would happen in the service that evening). Many times I would see particular individuals in detail, even the clothes they would be wearing, where they would be seated, what was physically (and sometimes spiritually) wrong with them; and I would hear what God wanted me to say to them and how He wanted to minister to them. Often, in order to confirm what God had said, I shared these prophetiic insights with my wife or the host pastor before service—and *NEVER EVEN ONCE, DID ANY VISION EVER FAIL TO COME TO PASS!!*

Since I recognized the conditions which were prevalent when the realm of (S)spirit opened to me, the question naturally arose: if I could facilitate the physical and mental conditions (deep relaxation and tranquility), would it follow that the dimension of (S)spirit would become more readily accessible? After countless personal meditation sessions my answer to that question is a resounding, "Yes!"

Let me restate that this often happens naturally and unintentionally. I frequently observe Christians entering into the presence of the Holy Spirit during worship services while sitting serenely with eyes closed, hands in their laps and faces raised and aglow. They are simply doing what enables *them* to tune out their *physical* surroundings and to enter the realm of (S)spirit. They are, in fact practicing a form of meditation, although they are probably unaware that this is what they are doing.

Some believe it is all right to enter the state I have described and have spiritual experiences—as long as it happens *spontaneously*. They seem to feel it is wrong to have an understanding as to "how" and "why" certain spiritual events occur. That reasoning is akin to equating spirituality with ignorance and, if that be so, I know a few *very* spiritual people! Let me state again emphatically, that the major function of this book (and my seminars) is to enable Christians, with knowledge and by design, to enter the dimension of (S)spirit and to cause supernatural things to transpire in their lives by becoming thus yielded to the Holy Spirit! To quote the words of the Apostle Paul, "Now concerning spiritual gifts, brethren, *I do not want you to be unaware*" (ignorant; I Cor. 12:1; emphasis mine.)

Music—A Gateway To The Spirit

In II Kings 3:13-20 the kings of Israel and Judah desperately needed guidance from the Lord, so they sought out the prophet Elisha. In verse fifteen Elisha said, "'But now bring me a minstrel.' And it came about *when the minstrel played that the hand of the Lord came upon him.*"

We know that *God* doesn't need anything, let alone music to work His wonders—to think so would be absurd. It was the *prophet* who needed some assistance! Music helped bring about the right frame of mind—a tranquil, reflective, meditative reverie so he could become receptive to what God was saying.

Please read the narrative in I Samuel 16:14-23. It concerns an evil spirit which would often come upon King Saul and would not leave until anointed music was played. Music, as an adjunct to spiritual experiences, must have been an accepted practice among the Jews because upon seeing Saul's tormented condition, his companions' first reaction was, as recorded in verse sixteen:

> Let our lord (the king, ed.) now command your servants who are before you. Let them seek a man who is a skillful player on the harp; *and it shall come about when the evil spirit from God is upon you, that he shall play the harp with his hand, and you shall be well.*

So they went out and found David, who would later become king. In verse twenty-three it says:

> So it came about whenever the evil spirit from God came to Saul, *David would take the harp and play with his hand*; and Saul would be refreshed and be well, *and the evil spirit would depart from him.* (Emphasis mine.)

I will not deal with this topic in depth here, except to say that there is a definite anointing in music; either Godly or Satanic; good or bad; uplifting or depressing; warming or chilling. How often we have heard the expression, "Music stirs the chords of the soul," or "Music soothes the savage breast"—and it does. Music has always held a fascination for man. Since it ministered to him on a *subliminal* level He might not have been able to explain in technical language what was happening (spiritually) within him, but he was able to associate it with the playing of music.

Why do you suppose it is that we most often witness a manifestation of gifts of the Holy Spirit in our worship services following worshipful singing and playing? Very simply because *music serves as a gateway to the (S)spirit.*

Having studied the narrative of Saul's deliverance from an evil spirit, I believe his own spirit was so elevated by the anointing accompanying David's skillful playing, that an evil entity could not abide in that holy atmosphere, and simply would not stay! Music is definitely *one* means by which our souls can be elevated to touch the spiritual dimension.

Spiritual Supermen?

There may be some readers who feel that the life of the (S)spirit-led person or the kinds of prophetic ministries we have been referring to are reserved for some *elite* number of spiritual supermen—if so, you are mistaken! Listen to the response of Moses to those in his day who labored under the same false impression. A young man came rushing up to him, reporting that, "...Eldad and Medad are prophesying in the camp." Joshua responded immediately (obviously not waiting for a word from the Lord) and, *speaking on his own initiative* demanded, "Moses, my lord, restrain them." This demonstrates that even great religious leaders don't always have the mind of the Lord, and sometimes speak on their own accord! Listen to the thoughts which probably crowded Joshua's mind that morning:

> "If we allow these two to get away with prophesying today, who knows how many will be doing it tomorrow? *Moses* is God's *chosen, hand-picked prophet*, and no one but *he* hears from God. This could get out of hand, and soon *everyone* will think that he can do the same thing."

I love Moses' reply: "Are you jealous for *my* sake? *Would that ALL the Lord's people were prophets, that the Lord would put His Spirit upon them!*" (Num. 11:27-30; emphasis mine.)

Many years later Moses' desire was fulfilled, and it began on the Day of Pentecost when, "...they were *all* filled with the Holy Spirit and began to speak with other tongues, as the Spirit was giving them utterance." (Acts 2:4; emphasis mine.) God continued in the early church to honor the desire of Moses, as reflected in the words of Paul:

...When you assemble, *each one* has a psalm, has a teaching, has a revelation, has a tongue has an interpretation...for *you can all prophesy* one by one, so that all may learn and all may be exhorted. (I Cor. 14:26,31; emphasis mine.)

It is clearly God's desire that *every* Spirit filled believer be able to minister to others via the gifts of the Holy Spirit, *but especially through prophecy.*

Of course, we recognize that this is not the case—most believers have no continuing manifestations of the gifts of the Holy Spirit in their lives. What a pity! For some, this lack is due solely to an absence of concern or desire, disregarding the commandment of the Apostle Paul to "...desire *(covet,* ed.), earnestly spiritual gifts, *but especially that you may prophesy."* (I Cor. 14:1b; emphasis mine.) For most, however, the dearth of spiritual gifts is due to a lack of information or teaching from the pulpit, rather than to a disregard for the Word of God. Preachers cannot teach what they know little or nothing about themselves, and that is most often the case. Jesus referred to a similar situation as "...the blind leading the blind."

Paul began his treatise on the gifts of the Holy Spirit in I Corinthians 12:1 with these words, "Now concerning spiritual gifts, brethren, *I do not want you to be unaware* (ignorant, ed.)." Please understand that those who fill our pulpits today are those who were seated in the pews not so many yesterdays ago, being trained by someone who may have known little, if anything about the gifts of the Holy Spirit. Then they went to seminary (perhaps the word is *cemetery!)* and were trained for ministry by someone who had sat in a pew and been taught by someone who knew little....! I think you can see the picture of a cycle which is difficult to break.

Sometimes we are trained to think we have *all* the right answers and have *none* because our answers are man-made. The cycle *can* be broken, and we *can* get off the treadmill of ignorance concerning the gifts of the Holy Spirit. Breaking the cycle begins with a sense of need, and grows until it becomes a burning, consuming, passionate desire. Then, and only then, can you proceed on the road to spiritual insight and Holy Spirit power!

Most people who would like to function in the gifts of the Holy Spirit are patiently waiting for the gift to somehow "take them over" and "manipulate" them—anticipating something completely beyond their control. That is what we refer to as the "seizure mentality"; when someone expects to be seized by some external power which will captivate their will, mind and body. If that is what you have been looking forward to, my sincere advice is to *stop waiting*, since it will only lead to greater frustration and more precious time wasted.

What *is* needed is a spiritual sensitivity to the realm in which the gifts operate—the dimension of (S)spirit. When you recognize that there is something *you* must do to precipitate spiritual perception you will be well on your way to functioning in that realm. Countless numbers of precious believers have failed to receive the baptism in the Holy Spirit with speaking in other tongues, simply because they were waiting for the Holy Spirit to take them over and do the talking for them, when that is not what occurs at all. Acts 2:4 says quite explicitly, "...and *they began to speak with other tongues* as the Spirit was giving them utterance." (Emphasis mine.) The Spirit gave the words—but *they* did the speaking. Once they were enlightened as to their responsibility, I have led as many as eighty-five people in a single service, into the experience of being filled with the Holy Spirit, speaking in other tongues. Being able to function in the gifts of the Holy Spirit requires similar yieldedness.

Let us examine spiritual gifts in the light of their Greek meanings. The word for "spiritual" is *pneumatikos* (from *pneuma*, "pertaining to spirit")—in this case, referring to the gifts of the Holy Spirit. The word for "gifts" is *charisma,* derived from the root word *charis,* from which we get the word "grace" (a free bestowment of God upon someone who is unworthy). So, from this we learn that the gifts are emanations of the presence of God's grace in our lives. But we must not think that they are like Christmas presents, all tied up with a bow and handed to us. Rather, they are *abilities of the (S)spirit*—the actual translation for gifts being "spiritual endowment; *miraculous faculty."*

I cannot emphasize strongly enough that, at the "new birth," man's spirit is born into God's Spirit; and Scripture emphatically states that our spirits and His are now MERGED INTO *ONE!:* "But he that is joined unto the Lord *is one spirit..."* (I Cor. 6:17; emphasis mine.)

If we could understand what the Spirit of Jesus is like, we would then have an appreciation for what He has given *us* the potential to become, (since we are now *one spirit).* Let us examine that subject in the light of what the Scriptures reveal to us about Him.

Jesus knew at all times what was transpiring in the realm of Spirit!

> Jesus therefore answered and was saying to them, "Truly, truly, I say to you, the Son can do nothing of Himself, *unless it is something He sees the Father doing*; for whatever the Father does,

these things the Son also does in like manner (in the same way, ed.) For the Father loves the Son, and *shows Him all things that He Himself is doing* and greater works than these will He show Him, that you may marvel...*I can do nothing on My own initiative.* As I hear I judge..." (Jn. 5:19,30a; emphasis mine.)

Jesus therefore said... *"I do nothing on My own initiative,* but I speak these things as the Father taught Me." (Jn. 8:28b; emphasis mine.)

Jesus said the Father showed Him *all* things that He Himself was doing—then Jesus performed on earth what was happening in the dimension of (S)spirit. Our primary—no, our *single* goal in life should be to become as yielded and sensitive to things of the Father (Spirit) as Jesus was. Then every day would be lived in faith and the confidence that we were moving in God's perfect will.

The same degree of yieldedness that was manifested in the life of Jesus, is required of us if we want to see identical miraculous results in our own ministries. Our lives will produce supernatural effects commensurate to the extent that we yield ourselves to experience the (S)spirit which God has placed within us.

18

DELEGATED AUTHORITY

One of the first lessons to be learned is that certain aspects of the gifts of the Holy Spirit are placed within *our* purview. This concept will seem strange to some readers, but it has *strong* Scriptural support! Since this book is not devoted primarily to teaching on the gifts of the Holy Spirit, I cannot consume the space this topic deserves—but we will consider a few verses which pertain to *our* part in the operation of the gifts:

And having summoned His twelve disciples, *He gave them authority over unclean spirits, to cast them out, and to heal every kind of sickness...*And as you go, preach, saying, "The kingdom of heaven is at hand"...Heal the sick, raise the dead, cleanse the lepers, cast out demons; freely you received, freely give. (Matt. 10:1,7,8.)

And He ordained twelve, that they should be with Him, and that He might send them forth to preach, *and to have power to heal sicknesses, and to cast out devils.* (Mk. 3:15.)

And these signs will accompany those who have believed: in My name they will cast out demons, they will speak with new tongues; they will pick up serpents, and if they drink any deadly poison it shall not hurt them; *they will lay hands on the sick, and they will recover.* (Mk 16:17,18.)

And He sent them out to proclaim the kingdom of God, and *to perform healing.* (Luke 9:2.)

And whatever city you enter, and they receive you...*heal those in it who are sick,* and say to them, "The kingdom of God has come near you"...And the seventy returned with joy, saying, "Lord, *even the demons are subject to us* in Your name." (Luke 10:8,9,17.)

But Peter said, "I do not possess silver and gold, *but what I do have I give to you:* In the name of Jesus Christ the Nazarene—*walk!*" And seizing him by the right hand, he raised him up; and immediately his feet and his ankles were strengthened. (Acts 3:6,7.)

> And it came about that the father of Publius was lying in bed afflicted with recurrent fever and dysentery; and Paul went in to see him and after he had prayed, he laid his hands on him *and healed him*. (Acts 28:8; emphasis in all the above scriptures mine.)

All of the above verses support the concept that the power of God has been delegated to believers, and those same people should be *using* that power to advance the kingdom of God. Take note of how often the kingdom of God is mentioned in context with delegated power to destroy the works of the enemy! If, as some say, the kingdom of God no longer exists, then the works of power which were always associated with it are no longer viable for today. We then possess no more than all other religions which *claim* nothing—and therefore *have* nothing! But such is definitely not the case at all.

By way of preparation for the following material, please read I Corinthians 14:26-33. As you will soon discover there is far more to these verses than is discernible on the surface. At first glance they appear to be no more than simple rules regarding the operation and control of the gifts of the Holy Spirit, but on closer examination we find much more food for thought.

In verses 27,28 we read:

> If any one (individual, ed.) speaks in a tongue it should be by two or at the most three, and each in turn, and let one interpret; *but if there be no interpreter, let him keep silent in the church; and let him speak to himself and to God*. (Emphasis mine.)

What you have just read are Divine regulations governing the use of the oral gifts in a worship service. Since God is certainly a God of order, we might expect that there *would* be supervision of one sort or another regarding the display of the gifts—or *should* we? Why should God place regulations upon Himself—or assign restrictions to Himself? If the message in tongues were *directly initiated* by the Holy Spirit, no controls were needed; to attempt to regulate God would be sacriligious! There would be no legitimate reason to restrict their usage, for verse thirty-eight tells us, "God is not a God of confusion"; so He would not operate the gifts in a confusing or contradictory manner. But *man* might do so—and obviously *had—hence the controls.*

At no time does the Apostle Paul dispute the genuineness of what was spoken in tongues, but he does offer firm *direction* so that it be done properly. He states that an *individual* may not give more than two or at the most, three messages in tongues in a single service.

Again, if the Holy Spirit were the *direct* initiator of these tongues it would be audacious to even *think* of limiting or otherwise regulating them. The Holy Spirit knows when to start and He knows when to stop, and He does not need even an Apostle Paul to instruct Him. "For who has known the mind of the Lord, *that he should instruct Him....?*" (I Cor. 2:16a; emphasis mine.) Instruction is God's job, and that is exactly what He was doing through the Apostle Paul—instructing the *Church* in their use of the gifts!

Paul also says, "...and let one interpret." (I Cor. 14:27) Can you imagine the confusion that would ensue if two or more people were trying to interpret at the same time? Yet if the Holy Spirit were the *direct initiator* of this gifts' operation, then He would not have given an interpretation to two or more people simultaneously, thus there would *be* no confusion.

Verse twenty-eight says, "But if there is no interpreter, let him *keep silent in the church; and let him speak to himself and to God.*" (Emphasis mine.) Paul never disputed the validity of the tongues in question (nor of the interpretation(s) in the previous verse), nor did he imply that there was anything spurious about them. He simply admonished the speaker that, if there were no interpreter present, to speak "to himself and to God." Wouldn't the Holy Spirit know whether or not an interpreter was present; and if so, would He inspire a message in tongues if there were none present? Obviously, He would not! This lends strong credence to the fact that the Holy Spirit is not the *direct initiator* of these, and other gifts (*faculties, abilities*), in a Spirit-filled believer.

Then there is verse twenty-nine: "And let two or three prophets speak...." Yet another "superfluous" regulation, if the Holy Spirit is the *direct initiator* of the prophets' words.

Let us consider further verses which I hope will help clarify this concept for you. "And the (regenerated, ed.) spirits of prophets *are subject to the prophets.*" (I Cor. 14:32; emphasis mine.) The word for "subject" means:

> To subordinate; to obey; be under (be, make) subject (to, unto), be (put) in subjection (to, under) submit self unto.

It does not say that the spirits of the prophets are subject to the Holy Spirit (although that should be an accepted fact!), but that the *prophet's spirit is subject to the prophet himself.* The word for prophet, as used here, means "a foreteller," i.e. one who sees into the future and relates what he sees to others—*his* spirit is subject to him!

Another restriction placed upon prophets is found in Romans 12:6:

> And since we have gifts that differ according to the grace given to us, let each exercise them accordingly: if prophecy (foretelling the future, ed.), *according to the proportion of his faith.* (Emphasis mine.)

According to this passage, a prophet's prophecies must never exceed the limitations of his faith—a needless enjoinder if all prophecies are *directly initiated* by the Holy Spirit. If every prophetic word is bestowed upon the prophet *directly* by the Holy Spirit, then what does the proportion (amount) of the prophet's faith have to do with it? The truth that is being conveyed here is that prophets with major faith should give major prophecies; prophets with minor faith should utter minor prophecies—and that is as it should be. We keep coming full-cycle to the same fact: believers have a distinct role to play in the manifestations of the gifts of the Holy Spirit. It is absolutely imperative that we discover what our role is—and then fill it!

Smith Wigglesworth, that great Apostle of Faith of the early Twentieth Century, who had one of the greatest ministries of healing and deliverance from demons, is quoted by one of his closest friends as having said, "If the Holy Ghost doesn't move me, *I move the Holy Ghost.*" That statement was thought to be irreverent by some, but may not have been at all when we examine what Scripture has to say on the subject.

In I Corinthians, chapter twelve, after listing all nine gifts of the Holy Spirit, Paul sums them up by saying in verse eleven, "But all these (Gifts of the Holy Spirit, ed.) *worketh that one and the selfsame Spirit....*" (KJV—Emphasis mine.) The word for "worketh" is *energeo* (which means, *to energize, or cause to operate),* which sheds a whole new light on how we should approach the gifts. We have previously held to the premise that the Holy Spirit energizes *us* with the manifestation of the gifts; when actually the *opposite* is true. When we move in the gifts, the Holy Spirit is energized or caused to operate in our midst. The Scriptures plainly teach that the gifts of the Holy Spirit are resident *in*, and controlled *by* Spirit-filled believers. This accounts for the seeming misuse of gifts by some, or the operation of a gift in the life of someone whose life-style does not fit the essential mold of Christianity. (In both instances, of course, the person involved will be accountable to God for his behavior.) Three illustrations may shed light here:

1. Elisha—the possible misuse of the prophet's gift.

> Then he (Elisha, ed.) went up from there to Bethel; and as he was going up by the way, young lads came out from the city and mocked him and said to him, "Go up, you bald head; go up you bald head!" When he looked behind him and saw them, he cursed them in the name (authority, ed.) of the Lord. Then two female bears came out of the woods and took forty-two lads of their number. (I Kings 2:23; emphasis mine.)

Since the prophet's life was not in jeopardy, there appear to be no mitigating circumstances for his drastic action, and it would seem that anger and pride became his motivation. Certainly a lesser punishment would have sufficed to teach the lads respect for a man of God. Obviously, prophets' words *do* carry awesome weight, and they *do* come to pass, whatever the circumstances.

2. Balaam—the prophet-for-hire. (Please read Numbers 22-24.)

King Balak desired the prophet Balaam to place a curse upon his enemy, Israel, and said to him, *"For I know that he whom you bless is blessed, and he whom you curse is cursed."* (22:6; emphasis mine.) He promised Balaam great honor if he would perform this favor, and the prophet finally consented to go with him. While on the journey to curse Israel, an angel appeared before the jackass upon which Balaam was riding. The prophet failed to see the heavenly visitor, but the jackass did! (Isn't there a lesson *we* can learn from that? If a *jackass* can experience a supernatural vision, why do *we* have such a difficult time accepting spiritual visitations? If a *jackass* can see visions, then there must be hope for some of *us*!)

Three times Balaam failed to see the angel, although the jackass did; and three times Balaam beat the animal to make it go forward; but it refused, seeing the angel standing with a sword in his hand. Finally, the Lord opened Balaam's eyes:

> And Balaam said to the angel of the Lord, "I have sinned, for I did not know that you were standing in the way against me. Now then, if it is displeasing to you, I will turn back." But the angel of

the Lord said to Balaam, "Go with the men, but you shall speak
only the word which I shall tell you...." (Emphasis mine.)

There is far more here than just an interesting story. At this point in
his life Balaam had become a "prophet-for-hire," one who was willing
to misuse his powers to curse the people of God. So what? After all, the
words of someone of that caliber shouldn't be of any consequence. His
prophetic words certainly wouldn't come to pass; so let him prattle
on—right? *WRONG!* God must have thought otherwise, because He
sent an angel to prevent the madness of the prophet from causing him to
speak out against Israel. Because of the extreme manner in which God so
strongly intervened, we must conclude that words spoken by this prophet—*words not given by God*—would have been fulfilled! The spirit of
the prophets is indeed subject to the prophets.

3. Caiaphas—the exercise of a divine office.

But a certain one of them, Caiaphas, who was high priest that
year, said to them, "You know nothing at all, nor do you take into
account that it is expedient for you that one man should die for the
people, and that the whole nation should not perish." Now this he
did not say on his own initiative; *but being high priest that year, he
prophesied* that Jesus was going to die for the nation; and not for
the nation only, but that He might also gather together into one the
children of God who are scattered abroad. So from that day on
they planned together to kill Him. (Jn. 11:49-53; emphasis mine.)

That prophecy was the "first nail" in the cross for Jesus, and considering this man Caiaphas brings up a most thought-provoking illustration. Here was a person who had his heart set to murder God's Son, to
destroy the Prince of Peace, to kill the Lamb of God—totally without
justification! He would, shortly thereafter, arrest Jesus without due process of Jewish law, and would convene an illegal nighttime trial. He
would disregard Jewish law which demanded that criers go through the
city streets shouting for anyone who could testify to the benefit of the accused. Contrary to law, those guarding Jesus were allowed to blindfold
Him, punch Him in the face and mock Him.

On top of all these travesties of "justice," Caiaphas suborned men
who gave perjured witness against Jesus; and even when their testimonies
were inconsistent, the charges were not dropped; neither was Jesus

released. Caiaphas was determined to shed the blood of that innocent Man, and the next day he would do so.

Less than twelve hours later he delivered Jesus to Pontius Pilate for crucifixion, one of the cruelest forms of death ever devised by man. Further, Caiaphas paid rabble rousers, who went among the people and stirred the hearts of the crowd for blood by yelling, "Crucify Him! Crucify Him!" Then, the gentle, loving Savior of the world was murdered—and Caiaphas played the lead role in the drama! *That is the same man* who had *prophesied* a few nights earlier!

How could that have been? This story seems to violate everything we have been taught about living righteously in order to be used of the Holy Spirit. The solution to this mystery is there in plain sight: "Now this he (Caiaphas, ed.) did not say on his own initiative; *but being high priest that year,* he prophesied..." (Jn. 11:51; emphasis mine.) Our natural inclination is to look at the man and his wicked actions; yet his prophesying had nothing to do with him as a person. God said it had to do with the fact of his *"...being high priest that year..."* In other words, God honored the *office* of high priest and *not* the high priest *himself!*

Romans 11:29 sheds more light on this, "For the *gifts and the calling of God are irrevocable."* The word for "gifts" translates:

> Spiritual endowment; miraculous *faculty.* (The dictionary defines "faculty" as *"power of the mind* or body; ability. Power to do a special thing, *especially a power of the mind.* Power or privilege conferred; license; authorization.")

When these gifts begin to function we are endowed with a miraculous faculty which enables us to move in the dimension of the Holy Spirit. According to Scripture they are "irrevocable," which means God *never* takes them back! Once people learn to tap into the realm of (S)spirit, that knowledge is a part of them for life.

Timothy (a young preacher in the New Testament), had received such a gift (charisma, miraculous *faculty)* by the laying on of the Apostle Paul's hands. In I Timothy 4:14, Paul wrote to Timothy and admonished him, "Do not neglect the spiritual gift within you...." The word for "neglect" means "to be careless of: make light of; not regard." (This seems to be the situation in many of our churches today, where preachers and parishioners alike have little regard for the manifestation of the gifts in their midst.) Obviously, Paul's warning went unheeded and, for some reason unknown to us, Timothy *did* neglect the use of this *charisma.* It became dormant—*but it was still resident within him!*

In Paul's second letter to Timothy he wrote:

> For I am mindful of the sincere faith within you...and for this reason I remind you to *kindle afresh the gift of God* (miraculous faculty, ed.) which is in you.... (II Tim. 5a,6; emphasis mine.)

The King James Version says, "Stir up the gift...." The Greek implies, "the fanning of an ember until it bursts into flame again." Once more the Scriptures remind us that the individual has a distinct obligation to tend to the gift within him, without which "tending" the gift will not operate.

Peter says:

> As each one has received a special gift (*charisma,* miraculous *faculty), employ it* in serving one another, as good stewards of the manifold grace of God. (I Pet. 4:10; emphasis mine.)

The word for "employ" is derived from a Greek word which means "deacon, or servant." Peter was actually implying that the gifts are ours for the purpose of serving the Body of Christ, the Church—to minister to the sick and afflicted and to let the oppressed go free! The word "steward" means "a house distributor; manager, overseer," and was a term well understood by everyone in those days. Stewards worked as managers in the houses of the wealthy and, as such were in charge of all disbursements, distributing the wealth in the best interests of the household. As one might expect, it was a position of great power, great authority and great responsibility! Peter said that we are to be "distributors, managers and overseers of the manifold (diverse) grace (*charis,* root word for charismas, gifts) of God."

Paul said:

> And since we have gifts (charismas, miraculous *faculties)* that differ according to the grace (*charis*) given unto us, let each exercise them accordingly: if prophecy, *according to the proportion of his faith.* (Rom. 12:6; emphasis mine.)

We will deal later with the issue of faith in depth, since it is a major factor in the operation of the gifts.

Through *Christian Meditation,* we are enabled to enter the dimension of spirit and, through repeated practice, we begin to recognize His voice, and become increasingly sensitive to the presence and mind of the (S)spirit within us! Faith has to do with believing—believing has to do with knowing—and knowing has to do with seeing. All of these are (S)spiritual faculties which can, and should be developed. When I mention *seeing*, my reference is not to physical sight, but "seeing into the kingdom of God," as Jesus did, ascertaining what the Father is doing. When God's will in a given circumstance has been established (through meditation, by seeing the Father at work), it naturally follows that we can believe in our souls (minds) for the expected outcome.

Once the natural mind is in accord with the inner man of the (S)spirit (having ceased its open hostility and opposition to things of the (S)spirit) faith (super)naturally arises and a gift (miraculous *faculty)* is set into operation. Yes, *we* caused the gift within to function, but *it was not ours to select what would happen!* Our part was to simply elect to find the "mind of the Spirit" and fulfill it, as Jesus said He did! Once having seen or heard the will of God, we can then enact it. We do the actions—*the Holy Spirit is the motivating force behind, in front of, above and under all that we do!*

Of course, not everyone is conscientious and Scripture bears out that it is possible for people to use and even *misuse* the gifts (miraculous *faculties)* without the anointing. This fact is driven home quite powerfully in Matthew 7:22,23:

> Many will say to Me on that day, "Lord, Lord, did we not prophesy in your name, and in your name cast out demons, and in your name perform many miracles?" And then I will declare to them, "I never knew you; depart from me, *you who practice lawlessness."* (Emphasis mine.)

These verses tie in textually with Matthew 13:36-43, which I quoted earlier. Notice how they dovetail with verse forty-one:

> The Son of Man will send forth His angels, and they will gather *out of His kingdom* all stumbling blocks (everything that is offensive, ed.), and *those who commit lawlessness.* (Emphasis mine.)

(The word for "lawlessness" is *anomia* which means "in violation of law!")

Take note that Jesus did not refute the grandiose claims made by this company of people—of prophesying, casting out demons or the performance of "many miracles." They are simply and unceremoniously *cast out of the kingdom,* with the denunciation that they were *"IN VIOLATION OF LAW!"* These lawbreakers had been operating in a kingdom from which they had been prohibited and utilizing powers to which they had no *legal* rights. For this God ultimately judged them harshly! *POINT MADE—CASE CLOSED!*

19

SCIENCE *VS* THE HOLY SPIRIT, OR SCIENCE *AND* THE HOLY SPIRIT

It is obvious that for centuries there has been a wide gap between the institutional church and science, the cause of which should be no mystery. Toward the end of the Dark Ages man began to look beyond the narrow confines of his limited view of the cosmos as it had been presented to him by the "ecclesiastical" fathers. The minds of men of science were expanding with new thoughts, new horizons, new possibilities and new concepts—*which generated new questions.* For the first time they entertained possibilities which had never been discussed before—at least not *publicly.* Until this time it was the domain of the "ecclesiastical" church to publish all that men were allowed to know about their world or the universe. Deviation from that belief structure was tantamount to heresy—and heretics were dealt with harshly. Bodies of "heretics" were permanently mutilated—tongues were cut out for uttering thoughts not approved by the "ecclesiasticals"; eyes were plucked from their sockets for looking into new concepts without approval of the "ecclesiasticals;" countless others were boiled in oil, burned at the stake or otherwise physically dispatched by the "ecclesiasticals."

Of course, there were perfectly "valid" reasons why these atrocities were perpetrated upon these "heretics" who dared to investigate "non-ecclesiastically-approved" concepts. Some of these "heretics" actually believed that the world was *round* and *not flat* as the "ecclesiasticals" had taught. Galileo in fact, ventured to teach that the *sun*, and *not the earth* was the center of our universe; that the earth rotated around the sun and not vice versa, as the "ecclesiasticals" had taught. Consequently, this belief was considered absolute heresy. The "ecclesiasticals" also "knew", and taught that there was nothing beyond our galaxy—until development and use of the telescope proved otherwise.

And so the "ecclesiastical" church and the new field of science locked horns in a conflict which would endure for centuries. Of course we shouldn't necessarily fault the "ecclesiasticals" for their failure to investigate these new claims of science—that would have taken precious time from some of the truly "important" issues of theology which commanded their attention—issues such as: "How many angels can dance on the head of a pin?" Or the equally compelling, "Do animals have souls?" Then there was the greatest question of all: "Can God create a rock so big that even *He* can't lift it?" (This would actually be comical—if it were not so pathetically sad!)

These are only a few of the nonsensical absurdities which were actually considered great controversial theological issues, absorbing the attention of many of the leading "ecclesiasticals" of that era. With swelling numbers of "heretics" waiting in line to have their tongues cut off or their eyes plucked out; to be stretched on the rack, boiled in oil and burned at the stake—it is completely understandable that the "ecclesiasticals" had no time to explore the validity of scientific claims! (I hope you understand the facetious manner in which I write this with tongue-in-cheek; since there is *nothing* "understandable" about it at all!) What is *completely* understandable is the reason why, for centures the world of science has *hated* the "ecclesiastical" church!

Don't you rejoice that there aren't any people like those closed-minded "ecclesiasticals" around today? Isn't it wonderful that we have escaped from the narrow confines of the Dark Ages and the church is enlightened today—*or is it?* I truly wish that were so, but I'm afraid that is *not* the case. Many have not strayed far (if at all) from the closed mentality which burned "heretics" at the stake! My prayer is that we who claim to follow after truth, will always maintain the Berean attitude of "...*examining the Scriptures daily, to see whether these things were so.*" (Acts 17:10-12; emphasis mine.)

If the "ecclesiastical" church had held sway we would still be living in the dark ages, literally—not even having electricity to light our homes. It is my firm belief that *true* science and the Bible are not in conflict—rather, being totally compatible they compliment one another. Scientists do not create they simply *discover* God's laws which have been in effect (through perhaps unknown to men) since creation—then devise ways to harness these creative forces for the benefit of mankind. Yes these forces can be misused (witness the use of atomic energy as a destructive power), but those who do so will answer to the Creator for their actions.

Perhaps it would be profitable to reflect momentarily on certain (S)spiritual experiences in the light of scientific scrutiny. It has often been said, "You can't put God in a test tube" and that would seem to be a logical conclusion, since even the infinite universe cannot contain Him. However, that statement is true *only* in the sense that you cannot bring God ionto the laboratory, break Him down into His component parts, analyze Him, and then *understand* Him. But who would question the fact that certain noticeable (and often *measurable*) physiological changes take place in a person when under the influence of the Holy Spirit; changes such as an increase in respiration or heart rate; while others experience a great warmth or shivers, sometimes accompanied by "goosebumps." So, though it is true that we can't analyze God we can observe any physical changes which take place in His children during (S)spiritual experiences. To do this we must, of necessity, turn to the world of science, and consider the principle of "cause and effect."

A flourescent light bulb can easily be illuminated while being held in your hand, without being connected to any power source. By simply placing it within an electronic force field it will light up as if by magic. The force field itself is *invisible*, yet its *effects* can be readily observed as the bulb glows brightly.

Countless other scientific experiments would, by their redundancy, only confirm the same fact, under certain controlled circumstances the effects of the invisible world of force fields can be observed. By using the same principle of "cause and effect," we may be able to learn certain interesting and important facts about the (physically) *invisible* world of the (S)spirit by observing certain *visible effects*. I humbly ask you to reserve judgment until you have completed this portion of my book. Remember—*there is no sin in maintaining an open mind*, but God may well consider it a breach of His trust, when we close our minds to the possibility of truth, which Jesus said "...will set you free."

The Invisible World of Brain Waves...Made Visible

Let's consider now the mysterious realm of brain waves and their possible correlation to *Christian Meditation*. The brain is a labyrinthine beehive of *constant* electrical activity, continually buzzing with thoughts; but until the advent of the electroencephalograph, no one could say with any certainty how it functioned. The electroencephalograph (e.e.g.) is an electronic device which can sense and measure the electrical activity (impulses) given off by the brain. These impulses are called "brain waves." There are four known, measurable brain waves: 1. Alpha, 2. Beta, 3. Theta, 4. Delta. They are measured, as is all electrical activity, in cycles per second (c.p.s.)

When one is awake and physically or mentally active, the brain is usually functioning in beta—somewhere between 14-21 (or more) c.p.s. (the "norm" being approximately 20 c.p.s.). This frequency is associated with man's *physical* being and the five senses, as well as active, rational, conscious thinking and reasoning.

Frequencies between 7-14 c.p.s. are known as alpha waves. At this level we experience daydreams during our waking hours and dreams while sleeping.

Frequencies between 4-7 c.p.s. are called theta waves. At this level of brain activity, one is more aware of *the inner being, the spiritual self and mind (soul)*, than of the *physical* self (the five senses and the time/space dimensions which surround the body). Theta waves are usually associated with the trance state.

Frequencies below 4 c.p.s. are referred to as delta waves and are associated with unconsciousness and the deepest levels of sleep. As of this writing, very little is known about them.

Two Halves Make A Whole

The brain is divided into two major parts, the "right and left hemispheres." Each has its own distinctly different functions. The left hemisphere operates in the realms of spoken language, reading and reasoning and is the intellectual, more rational side of the brain. The right hemisphere functions in the realms of body control, music awareness, three-dimensional forms, art awareness, *intuition* and *imagination.* It is obvious that the left hemisphere's primary concern is with analytical operations, while the right hemisphere's occupation is in the area of the *visionary and intuitive.* Roger Sperry, noted for winning the Nobel Prize for his split-brain research, discovered that when people had their brain hemispheres separated surgically, they responded to external stimuli in different ways. Their left hemispheres were able to describe things verbally but not by shape or touch. Conversely, using their right hemispheres it was possible for them to recognize shapes and general impresions, but not to ascribe names to them.

Psychological surveys indicate that a surprising *ninety-five percent* of people interviewed *leaned heavily toward left brain functions,* lending strong credence to my expanding conviction that we are cultivating a worship of the intellect. A recent study showed that all pre-schoolers showed some degree of what the investigators called E.S.P. (extra sensory perception or *intuition.*) They continued to observe these same children over a period of years, and it was discovered that the older they grew the less they manifested spontaneous intuition. It was concluded by the researchers that these children became more guarded in their thought-lives, as they were trained to "keep your thoughts to yourselves," etc.

The right hemisphere matures intellectually to approximately the 5-7 year old level (which may be one reason why creative people are often so childlike), although it may achieve the scale of genius in creative, artistic or intuitive spheres. This may indicate why children within that age bracket respond intuitively to a higher degree than older children or adults. Their left (intellectual) hemispheres have not matured beyond their right (intuitive) hemispheres; producing a harmony and interaction between the two which is often lost as the *intellectual left "outgrows" the intuitive right.* We "grow up," and in the process "grow out of" intuitive sensitivity! Perhaps this is partially what Jesus had in mind when He said:

> ...truly, I say to you, unless you are converted *and become like children* you shall not enter the kingdom of heaven. (Matt. 18:3; emphasis mine.)

My conviction, born out of years of experience is that, even though we may have "grown out of" intuitive sensitivity, we can and should, *relearn it* through *Christian Meditation.*

Scientists have also discovered that the left hemisphere actually grows slightly larger than the right hemisphere during schooling years, because the (rational, intellectual, reasoning) left half is exercised more than the (creative, visionary and intuitive) right half during that period. All *too* often the rational, reasoning, intellectually-oriented left hemisphere of the brain asserts itself to the point of *dominance,* subordinating the right hemisphere and *inhibiting* the flow of intuitive and imaginative thought out of which often proceed the revelations of the Holy Spirit. It is wrong to assume that each hemisphere of the brain operates independently of the other—they were designed to work in harmony as a *unit.*

When Jesus spoke of the "heart" He was not referring to the physical *organ,* but rather to man's *inner being;* so it is conceivable that He was alluding to the right hemisphere of the brain. This premise is born out by the fact that *all* the attributes He ascribed to the "heart" we *know* to be functions of the right hemisphere of the brain—such as dreams, visions, God's intuitive voice, creativity, etc. Further research leads me to the conclusion that there is a *distinct* correlation between the right hemisphere and the deepest level in man—his (S)spirit; and an equal correlation between the left hemisphere and man's rational, intellectual self. This would lead to the logical conclusion that the brain (mind), *especially* the right hemisphere is the intermediary (or bridge) between (S)spirit and intellect.

When Elisha wanted to receive a word from the Lord, he called for a minstrel to assist him in quieting his intellectual, reasoning mind and enable him to enter into a *state of mind* (soul) which was receptive to the Holy Spirit: *"...and it came about, when the minstrel played, that the hand of the Lord came upon him."* (II Kings 3:15; emphasis mine.)

Left hemisphere functions are usually accompanied by higher cycles per second—in the *beta* wave range. Ninety-five percent of all human beings spend most of their waking hours in that range of brain wave activity. However, there are times when the dominance of this one hemisphere can actually be a *liability* rather than an *asset*. For instance, sometimes an *intuitive insight* (right brain function) will contradict *logic* (left brain function). At such times, the intuitive is often *suppressed* in favor of *logic,* only to discover later that *intuition* was correct. It is realy no mystery then, why there are *so few prophets and seers* in the Twentieth Century "ecclesiastical" church, which seems to have truly become a "Non-*Prophet* Organization!"

The Answer Is Blowing In The Wind

Contemporary society has *cultivated* the *intellectual* and often *spurned* the *creative, intuitive and mystical* aspects of personality; something which more primitive cultures have not had the option of doing. People who live in simpler societies use *both* sides of the brain with equal facility. Canadian Mounties in remote areas have often been fully informed by Eskimo helpers of tragic events happening many miles away, events which were verified in every detail months later. Careful checking revealed the astonishing fact that *the information often arrived immediately after the distant event transpired*, long before any physical message could possibly have gotten through. When asked to explain how they knew these things, the natives replied, *"It's the wind."* They could not articulate the source of the impressions, but *they accepted them as natural occurrences.*

I find it intriguing that the source of this extra-sensory knowledge was expressed as being simply "the wind." In both the Old and New Testaments the word translated *spirit* is "wind." In the Old Testament the Hebrew word is *ruwach;* and in the New Testament it is the Greek *pneuma.* The advent of the Holy Spirit on the day of Pentecost was occasioned by "...a noise like a violent, rushing wind...." (Acts 2:2)

Similar reports have come from the Outback of Australia, where government agents have related nearly identical incidents among the aborigines as those cited concerning the Eskimos. Such happenings are by no means indigenous to only these two peoples, but are widespread throughout the world. The one common thread which binds all of these events together is that they happen to people whose left brain hemispheres are not overly developed *intellectually* and who have need, by virtue of their environment, of the *intuitive and instinctual* information provided by the right brain hemisphere! Since they have no better explanation, the "ecclesiasticals" write these happenings off in their favorite "catchall" categories of "nonsense" or "demonic activity."

It should not be misconstrued that such things occur only among the *illiterate* or the *simple* of the world. I cite them as perfect examples only because they have no intellectual barriers to hinder the intuitive realm as "civilized" man often does. Yet in fact, the exact opposite can also be true, since much genius is often a balance between the intellectual and the intuitive. Johann Sebastian Bach, composer of classical music, was quoted as stating that he felt the magnificent musical compositions he wrote were not his own work, since he actually *heard* the music in his head and simply recorded the notes on paper. This indicates a strong leaning towards right brain thinking, with full freedom of informational movement from the right side of the brain to the left.

How quickly some would judge these happenings as being evil—but if we wish to understand the things of the (S)spirit we must be slow to judge and swift to learn, remembering that however our brains (minds, souls) function, it is because *GOD* created them that way! If we believe that the right brain is the "heart" alluded to in Scripture, then we should learn all we can about it and discover how to employ it for our own benefit and that of others. As with any journey, there may be more than one road—but in this book and in my seminars we are examing what many fine born-again Christians consider to be the most direct route to the inner being—*Christian Meditation!*

Getting To The "Heart" Of The Matter

Having already broached the subject of the various brain waves (alpha, beta, theta and delta) I would like to explore their relevance to *Christian Meditation* and reaching the inner man of the heart (mind).

The human brain, while in the waking state, operates in beta at approximately 20 c.p.s., since this is where the left hemisphere's functions of logic and reasoning operate best. We also have many flashes of alpha waves every minute, each of which last only milli-seconds. However, during moments of reverie, such as daydreaming, alpha becomes the dominant wave and brain activity may drop down to 10 c.p.s. Psychologists have discovered it is at this level of brainwave activity that our minds accept suggestion most readily. Thus, learning how to stimulate alpa waves is of great importance in "renewing the mind," programming it with God's Word. (Operating at that level also has beneficial *physical* side affects, since the body seems to speed up its healing process at 10 c.p.s.) Yet, most important of all, at 10 c.p.s. we begin to gain access to the right brain hemisphere—the area which I believe is referred to in Scripture as the "inner man of the heart"—the *bridge* which spans the gap between soul and (S)spirit. If we desire to become more (S)spiritually intuitive, and since this ability increases and functions more effectively at 10 c.p.s., then we should seek to function more often at that level. *Christian Meditation*, as taught in my seminars, will help you accomplish that goal.

If you can *think of* the right hemisphere (the inner man of the heart) as an intermediary (a missing link or *bridge* between your conscious mind and your (S)spirit), you will understand the need to learn how to reach it. Allow me to illustrate this bridge concept:

The Holy Spirit had led me to schedule an evangelistic crusade in Argentina. While I was making preparations to go, my contact in that country wrote me with the distressing news that persecution of Christians had become epidemic in the area where I was to minister. Meetings were being broken up with tear gas and vicious attack dogs had been unleashed upon the crowds on two occassions. He himself had been arrested four times and was facing the possibility of four long prison terms. Needless to say, he advised me against coming into that atmosphere though the final decision would have to be mine. I honestly could not understand this turn of events, since I knew what the Holy Spirit had instructed me to do. Therefore, after committing this situation to God, I flew to Argentina.

Because of the overt persecution it was not possible to preach publicly, so my ministry was confined to about forty people in the courtyard of a believer's house. I could not be persuaded that God had led me multiplied thousands of miles to another country, in the midst of great political and religious upheaval and at *much* threat to my own safety, to engage in such a limited ministry. After the first service in that crowded courtyard, where the Holy Spirit moved powerfully in signs and wonders, I witnessed the hand of God at work on our behalf. I was approached by a rather unassuming looking lady who informed me that she was a personal friend of the governor and she would arrange for me to meet with him. To my amazement, I was contacted early the next morning and requested to be at the governor's office at ten AM that day! I received his undivided attention for over two hours while I explained the plight of local Christians who were being so grievously persecuted by the mayor. Tears ran down his cheeks as he listened attentively and then asked me to pray for him. Before I left he presented me with gifts reserved for visiting political dignitaries (I *am* an ambassador for Christ) and placed his private plane and pilot at my disposal and gave me complete liberty to preach openly.

Which brings us to the purpose of this illustration: what caused the turning point for us in that hotbed of persecution? There was an extremely powerful person who *alone* held the key to religious liberty in that region, and it was *imperative* that I contact him. I didn't even know who he *was*, let alone how I was to *reach* him, but he was the *bridge* to all that was necessary to bring salvation, healing and deliverance to thousands!

If you were presented with a set of circumstances similar to what I have just described, what would you do? Wouldn't you seek out the one capable of supplying you with answers? Of course you would! Your (S)spirit could be compared to the governor, who alone has all the solutions to your problems, and it is *imperative* that you learn how to tap into that realm. You will be captivated by a desire to venture into the dimension of (S)spirit when it becomes evident to you that a direct access to God's Spirit is attained *only* in that realm. May I remind you once more that "...he that is joined unto the Lord *is one spirit*" (I Cor. 6:17, K.J.V.; emphasis mine.), and that (S)spirit is within you.

Of course, the gap between (S)spirit and flesh is a broad one with no obvious bridge to span the chasm—but there *is* a bridge! Unfortunately, it is overlooked by most because it is not conspicuously displayed to the casual observer. I believe this link between the flesh and (S)spirit is the subconscious mind, resident in the right brain hemisphere. It has access to both the (S)spirit and our flesh, and is most easily accessed while the brain is operating in alpha (at about 10 c.p.s.); and we have discovered that alpha is most easily attained through worship, music and *meditation*.

"In The Spirit" In The Laboratory

Some years ago I cooperated in a fascinating (though revolutionary) experiment to see if there might be some correlation between alpha and being "in the (S)spirit." This controlled experiment was conducted while

I prayed for the sick. The object was to determine if any appreciable, *measurable*, biological or physiological changes took place in the "gifted person" who was praying for the sick when healing was actually in progress.

I was wired to an electroencephalograph (e.e.g.—a device which does not *produce*, but simply *measures* brain waves), and was asked to indicate when I sensed God's healing presence *("...the power of the Lord was present for Him to perform healing."* Luke 5:17b; emphasis mine.) Only then was I to minister to the sick person. The results were predictable. When I sensed the anointing of the Holy Spirit, *my brain waves recorded very strong and long-lasting bursts of alpha waves.* Several people reported being healed that day.

A similar experiment to that mentioned above was conducted in the early part of this century with the cooperation of Reverend John G. Lake. Lake possessed one of the greatest healing ministries since the church of the First Century. Over a five-year period more than 100,000 healings were recorded in the "Healing Rooms" of his church in Spokane, Washington.

Having studied science, Lake desired to understand all that he possibly could as to how God healed, and thus submitted himself to scientific scrutiny in the laboratory. He related, that after being wired to an electronic device (probably an e.e.g., ed.):

> I began to repeat things like the 23rd Psalm *to soothe the mind and reduce its vibrations to the lowest point*...My difficulty was that while reciting, I could not keep the Spirit from coming upon me...those in charge of the experiment said, "You are a phenomenon. *You have a wider mental range than any human being we have ever seen."*[1] (Emphasis mine.)

In the experiment that followed, a powerful X-ray machine with microscopic attachments was connected to his head to determine if there were any discernable action of the brain cells. The experiment continued:

> *First, I repeated Scriptures that were soothing—those calculated to reduce the action of the cortex cells to their lowest possible register*...The fires of God began to burn in my heart...The professors said, "...We cannot understand this, but the cortex cells expanded amazingly."[2] (Emphasis mine.)

Lake then asked for those conducting the experiment to bring someone with an inflamation of the bone so that he might pray for him; after which the doctors declared that every cell in the afflicted limb was responding.

Allow me to quote John G. Lake himself, concerning his opinion of what transpires when we pray:

> The Almighty God, by the Spirit, comes into your soul, *takes possession of your brain and manifests Himself in the cortex cells of your brain. When you wish and will, either consciously or unconsciously,* the fire of God—the power of God, that life of God, that nature of God—*is transmitted from the cortex cells of your brain* and throbs through your nerves down through your person, into every cell of your being—into every cell of your brain, your blood, your flesh, and your bone—into every square inch of your skin, until you are alive with God! That is divine healing.[3] (Italics in the original; bold highlights mine.)

It is my impression that Lake was, in fact, using a form of meditation—which was calculated to "...soothe the mind *and reduce its vibrations to the lowest point"* and "...those calculated *to reduce the action of the cortex cells to their lowest possible register"* thus enabling him to enter the dimension of (S)spirit.

What's It All About, "Alpha"?

By now it must be obvious to you that a quiet frame of mind and body is needful in achieving an "alpha state"—but why? It will be helpful if you can envision your brain as a marvelous, God-given computer, and all of your nerves as wires whose function it is to transmit information from various parts of your body to the "central computer." Every physical motion, stressed muscle, bodily function (even those controlled by the autonomic nervous system, such as heartbeat, respiration, etc.), audio-input (sounds), visual perception (sights) and emotional stress all communicate this information to the "computer" in myriads of electrical impulses. All of this input must be decoded, analyzed and properly acted upon, causing the "computer" to function in "beta," the brainwave which is most useful when awake, alert and functioning in the *physical* realm but which serves little purpose, and is often a hindrance, when we wish to enter the *(S)spiritual* dimension.

Tranquil surroundings, peaceful mind and a relaxed body serve to reduce the amount of physical input (electrical impulses) to the brain, allowing it to relax, at which time it enters the "alpha state." It is at this level of brain waves that we become sensitive to the fourth dimension of (S)spirit. Allow me to answer a question which some readers must be entertaining: "Will I *always* have to retire to some quiet surroundings and perform a meditative exercise in order to function in the dimension of (S)spirit?" An excellent question, to which the answer is a relieving "no." The periods of meditation are at first to enable you to learn what it "feels" like to be in alpha and, with repeated practice, *to produce the alpha state at will,* even while otherwise physically and mentally alert. Actually, this is the ultimate goal to be sought after as you meditate.

As I said earlier, the brain wave biofeedback machine did not *cause* alpha waves to occur, it simply *recorded* what was already happening. If our flesh-and-blood being reacts and responds to various invisible stimuli in the physical, material world, why should we think it strange that there is a subtle physiological change (such as a shift in brainwave frequencies) when we are in the (S)spirit? Conversely, I have proven through years of experience that we can, through a process of relaxation and mental quieting, achieve an "alpha state" and thus be in tune with our inner man. I consider this a state of being in the realm of (S)spirit. Thus, we do not *produce* His voice, but we do produce a *state* in which we can *hear* His voice.

In concluding this segment on alpha I would like to make it clear that, when in alpha, the mind is alert and aware of what is going on around you, and it is in this condition that we actively program our minds to conform to the Word of God. (That is not to say that renewing of the mind cannot take place at other frequencies, such as theta which is an even more effective brain wave level for that purpose.)

The deeper state of theta (4-7 c.p.s.) is to be desired since it is at this level that trances occur and visions are experienced. This state of mind takes somewhat longer to achieve and demands considerably more trust and yieldedness to the (S)spirit within us, but can be arrived at by most people with continued practice. As with most disciplines, there are three elements which make for success: *practice, practice and more practice!*

---

¹ John G. Lake, Adventures In God, (Harrison House, 1981) p. 28.
² Ibid., pp. 29,30.
³ Ibid., p. 31.

20

VISUALIZATION

Even as there are two components to prayer: 1. Us speaking to God, and 2. Meditating, or allowing God to speak to us; there are two aspects to meditation which make it complete: 1. Active and, 2. Quiescent. Throughout this book we have been dealing primarily with the second, or quiescent aspect, in which we quiet our bodies and our *always* overactive minds in order to hear the voice of the (S)spirit within. Now we must consider the equally important active role which must be undertaken in order to achieve (S)spiritual balance. The active role in meditation is visualization.

There is a fine line drawn between imagery and visualization. Imagery (imagination) consists mainly of *thoughts or ideas* as opposed to visualization which is *the ability to think in pictures*. With imagery our thoughts, ideas or mental pictures are rather vague whereas, upon learning to visualize, we are able to focus our attention and thus (mentally) see a strong, crisp, clear image projected within a localized region of the brain. Imagery is perhaps the oldest method of thought, and is the primary manner in which man still thinks today. We are often engaged in this manner of thinking, though usually unaware of it.

All our lives we have been held captive by the imagination, sometimes for our good, but more often to our detriment. Since imagination is such a potent force in our lives, it is imperative that we have a greater understanding, and *control*, of it. Psychologists have learned that when fact and imagination come into conflict, *imagination will invariably win out*.

Allow me to illustrate the strength of imagination when pitted against the power of fact:

> If I suspended a 2" x 12" plank, eight feet long, between two chairs and asked for volunteers to walk the length of it, probably everyone asked would be willing to do so. This is a simple task which almost anyone could accomplish easily. But consider what would happen if I took that same plank twenty stories high, placed it between two buildings and then asked the *same* people to walk across it. I would probably lose 99.9% of my volunteers! Why? It is the same plank, the same wood, the same strength, the same width, the same thickness. *Only the location has changed*—but is that really *all* that has changed? NO! Something else has been introduced—*imagination*.

What actually would take place during the twenty-story ascent to the rooftop is that imagination would run wild, conjuring up all sorts of "reasons" why it would be impossible to "walk the plank." Notice that all of the reasons share the root of *fear:* fear of height, fear of falling, fear of passing out, fear of the plank breaking, fear of losing your balance, fear of a wind blowing you off the plank...*fear, fear, fear—and all of it created by imagination!*

Our misuse of imagination can be readily traced back to our childhoods. For instance, as a child, why do you suppose you were afraid of the dark? Your fear was undoubtedly initiated by what you *imagined* it to contain. Imagination plays a large role in and governs much of our lives, dictating choices which often determine our destinies; yet most people have *absolutely no idea how to control it.*

Think of your brain as a computer and realize that much of what it "knows" has been programmed into it by your imagination (possibly with *no basis in fact*)—then you can understand why you act or react as you do in certain circumstances, or why particular experiences in life often frustrate you.

I once dined with a husband and wife who worked in the computer field and several times during the course of the evening, when speaking of their work, they used the term "GIGO" (pronounced jee-go). I hated to confess my ignorance, but curiosity won over my desire to appear informed, even though I wasn't. I finally asked the meaning of this mystery work "GIGO" and was told that it is an acronym used in computer language to convey *"Garbage In, Garbage Out."* In other words, a computer is no better than what is programmed into it. And the material programmed reflects the programmer—right or wrong, good or bad. Your mental computer is no different—*"Garbage In, Garbage Out"*; or conversely, *"Good In, Good Out"*; or even better yet, *"God In, God Out!"* The wonderful, mind-liberating fact is that we *do* have a choice concerning what goes in...and therefore what comes out of our minds!

Your thought-life governs your actions; therefore, where you are today is where the thoughts (imaginations) from all your yesterdays (whether good or bad) placed you—*and where you will spend all your tomorrows,* unless the course of your thought life is modified via your imagination. Since your outer person is a reflection of what your inner man believes, if you desire to change the course of your life, you will need to alter some of your errant beliefs.

All thought patters (beliefs), whether correct or not, have become established simply by thinking and/or saying them often enough; this is how habits are formed. Researchers have discovered that it takes approximately twenty-one days (three weeks) for the brain to form a neural pattern, otherwise known as a habit or conditioned reflex. It takes about the same amount of time to begin to *undo* it, depending on how long it has been rooted there. The old expression. "You can't teach an old dog new tricks" probably does apply to old dogs, but it just *isn't* so in the lives of humans! Remember, the renewing of the mind is *our* responsibility and we can choose, scripturally, those patterns of thing which we desire to embody—or wish to change, We can take on good characteristics, or shed bad ones, by consistent, careful and prayerful attention to our thought-life *through Christian Meditation and visualization.*

The computer (brain) was meant to serve us, but through a lack of information, and wrong programming, we have become enslaved by the servant, who is often a cruel taskmaster. Thoughts of fear, inadequacy or lack of self-control in the area of habits (smoking, drinking, overeating, lust, etc.) have bound many. But now there is hope! Through the proper use of *Christian Meditation,* we are able to *re*program (renew) our thought lives) by aligning our minds with what the Word of God says about us and to us) and experience the joy of transformation as referred to by the Apostle Paul in Romans 12:2b:

> *Be transformed by the renewing of your mind,* that you may prove what the will of God is, that which is good and acceptable and perfect (Emphasis mine.)

Throughout history there have been people who have learned to use imagination and visualization quite constructively, among whom are most notably inventors, artists, authors, research scientists, etc. These people have returned the God-given gift of imagination to its rightful place of subservience. Instead of being servant to, and at the mercy of an uncontrolled imagination, they have harnessed its abilities causing it to serve as a catalyst for illumination and invention. Out of this have come countless blessings for the betterment of mankind. By no means have all the aforementioned people been Christians; yet they have learned to utilize their wonderful, God-given gifts of imagination and creativity. Therefore how much greater should *our* contribution to mankind be—we who possess renewed minds, who experience a personal walk with the Creator of all things and are privy to the "mind of Christ" with all of its creative and inventive energies!

21

A PICTURE IS WORTH A THOUSAND WORDS

We Westerners have effectively succeeded in changing Christianity from a *relationship* to a *religion* and having done this, the institutional, "ecclesiastical church" finds itself lacking the dynamic energy which is brought about when Christians experience a close, interactive, Father-son union between God and man. In the sterile atmosphere thus produced, man speaks to God but God no longer answers him personally; neither does God intervene directly in individual affairs. Since, according to some "ecclesiasticals" there is nothing to see, it is therefore unnecessary to cultivate the faculty of visualization. Yet other factions agree that there *is* something to see—but we are forbidden to look into the realm of (S)spirit.

For many centuries this has been the case as the "ecclesiastical church" gradually moved farther and farther away from the supernatural and now worships at the "altar of intellect" which is established solely on *reason*. Along with the altar of intellect they have created an "ecclesiastical hierarchy," which at best is capable only of telling the congregation *about* God; when in fact the major theme of Scripture is that we are to *know* God personally, walking in intimate fellowship with Him, hearing His voice and experiencing His presence. Often, the church is nothing more than a club where we go to hear stories about the Bible.

Because *true* Christianity is a *mystical spirit-to-Spirit relationship* ("God is spirit; and those who worship Him must worship in spirit and truth." Jn. 4:24), it should be expected that the faculty of visualization would be much in use in our quest to experience God's presence. However, since we have profoundly Westernized Christianity, we now live in a world of intellectual and rational concepts when we should be moving in the supernatural realm of visions and dreams, which depend upon a sensitivity to (S)spiritual intuition. In order to re-establish a continuing contact with the realm of (S)spirit and enhance our affinity with God, we must learn to live in the dimension of visions and dreams.

That the God of our Lord Jesus Christ, the Father of glory, *may give you a spirit of wisdom and of revelation* in the knowledge of Him. I pray that the eyes of your heart (mind, ed.) may be enlightened, so that you may know what is the hope of His calling, what are the riches of the glory of His inheritance in the saints. (Eph. 1:17,18; emphasis mine.)

The word translated "heart" (in the King James Version, "understanding") is *dianoia,* "deep thought, the faculty (mind or its disposition), by implication; its exercise; *imagination.*" So the intent of the Apostle Paul's prayer was that the inner eyes of our *imaginations* may be enlightened; and I am convinced that this is one of the *primary* means by which God communicates His revelations to us.

Dr. Paul Yonggi Cho, pastor of the largest church in the history of Christianity (over a half million members), agrees with this concept. For even greater insight into this subject, please read Dr. Cho's book, "The Fourth Dimension," in which he states: *"The language of the Holy Spirit is the dream and vision."*

Watchman Nee, prolific writer of this century said: *"The picture is the Holy Spirit's memory."*

If one lacks an intense appreciation for the value of cultivating the inner man (his ability to visualize), he will not devote proper attention to it and little, if anything of a miraculous nature will transpire in his life. When we turn our attention toward visualization we are not embarking upon a novel pastime—but on a new way of life! When the words were penned, "Take time to be holy, speak oft' with thy Lord," the hymn writer understood that some things simply *cannot* be hurried.

Surveys have indicated that at least forty percent of the populace does not know how to visualize, while the remaining sixty percent do so with varying degrees of success. Since this ability has been so neglected in our society visualization must now be *re*learned. This is but one illustration of the manner in which neglect of the right brain's faculties has led to a diminishing of function. Some will have to work harder than others, but it is my firm conviction that *all* can learn.

In attaining the ability to visualize we are not seeking to produce our own visions or dreams, but to expedite the channel by which the Holy Spirit may convey His thoughts and revelations to us! (We must not use this faculty to create our own desires, but to enable us to move more fluidly in the dimension of (S)spirit once we have ascertained the will of God.)

While it is true that God uses us as we are, often "as we are" is not "as we *could* be;" therefore our availability or usefulness is limited accordingly.

A vivid illustration of this is found in the writing ministries of Luke and the Apostles Peter and Paul. It is true that God used them "as they were," but it becomes quite obvious, even upon casual observation of the original (Greek) New Testament manuscripts, that Paul had considerably more to offer educationally and intellectually than did Peter.

The Petrine epistles are limited not only in size (only two rather brief letters), but also in the *style* of writing; Peter used the "vulgar" (unrefined, "street language") Greek of his day. His lack of education is also highlighted by the amount of misspelled words and grammatical errors so prevalent in the original texts of I and II Peter—yet God used what Peter had to offer!

The Apostle Paul is the complete antithesis of Peter; he was well educated theologically ("at the feet of Gamaliel"), and he possessed the finest secular education his wealthy family could afford. He in turn authored thirteen of the twenty-seven books of the New Testament (fourteen, if he wrote Hebrews as some scholars believe). The Pauline epistles bear eloquent testimony to Paul's great learning, having been written in nearly flawless classical Greek (as are also the writings of Luke who composed two lengthy books, the Gospel of Luke and the Acts of the Apostles). God did not love Paul and Luke any more than He did Peter, yet in a literary sense—He found more to use in them! Little did they realize when they were being educated that the faculties being acquired would someday be the means through which the Holy Spirit would communicate God's Word to mankind.

This should serve to illustrate our need to expand our awareness and provide fertile soil in which the Holy Spirit can plant His seed! As with everything else in life, "practice makes perfect." Let me reiterate what I stated earlier, (and I cannot stress this strongly enough!) *WE DO NOT PRODUCE THE VISIONS AND DREAMS!* The more this facet of our being is yielded to the Holy Spirit, the better He can develop it as an avenue of access to *our* (S)spirits. The finest example of this ability is in the life and ministry of Jesus Christ who said:

> ...Truly truly, I say to you, the Son can do nothing of Himself, *unless it is something He sees the Father doing;* for whatever the Father does, these things the Son also does in like manner. For the Father loves the Son, *and shows Him all things that He Himself is doing*...(Jn. 5:19,20; emphasis mine.)

Since Jesus did *nothing* on His own initiative, but was *totally* dependent upon observing what was transpiring in the dimension of (S)spirit, and then fulfilling it—it becomes presumptuous for us to use any of the faculties of our (S)spirits in a manner inconsistent with His example. The aspiration of every Christian should be to emulate the life and ministry of Jesus in this regard. It is my firm conviction that we should not use visualization indiscriminately to create the fulfillment of our own desire. Rather, we should wait upon God in *Christian Meditation* to ascertain the will of the Holy Spirit; then, having determined "what the Father is doing," we can use visualization to bring it to fruition. The Psalmist declared, "Delight yourself in the Lord; *and He will give you the desires of your heart.*" (Ps. 37:4; emphasis mine.) This verse has often been misinterpreted to mean that "if you delight yourself in God, then He will give you anything you want." Not so! The word translated "delight" really means "to wallow in"—*to luxuriate in complete abandonment to God and His will!* Then, when you reach the state where you are totally enraptured with God (and surrendered to His will), *He will impart proper desires to you—His* desires will become *your* desires. The fact is that, having developed the faculty of visualization, we *facilitate* the means by which the Holy Spirit reveals the Father's activities to us.

All of life is a silent witness to the importance of man's desire (and therefore his need) to visualize. Most people prefer a novel which describes scenes and actions in vivid detail, drawing "word pictures" which cause us to mentally "see" the people, places and events portrayed. In the same way, our preference is usually television over radio for the same obvious reasons. Pictures move us far more than mere words, thus the oriental proverb: "A picture is worth a thousand words."

A perfect illustration in point and one with which we are all familiar:

A worthwhile charity sponsoring orphans in foreign, poverty-stricken lands where you have never been, wants to solicit financial support from you. Their appeal via radio describes the needs and the desperate plight of these poor suffering children in graphic "word pictures." These are intended to project an image on your mind which in turn touches your heart and opens your pocketbook. It works! But if the same charity uses television the appeal might be structured somewhat differently. A possible scenario:

Camera scans a scene of great poverty while a voice off camera recounts the desperate needs of the people. Then the camera singles out one child (usually a little girl about four years old), and slowly "pans in" on her until her hunger-stricken face fills your screen. Her large, brown, nearly expressionless eyes fill with tears which spill over and run down her cheeks. No words are spoken...*none have to be.* At this time a telephone number, which you can call to pledge your support, comes on the screen.

Is this type of appeal successful, and if so, is it more so than the purely verbal appeal of the radio? Ask the charity's promoters—their resounding "YES!" will prove that we are far more motivated *by images* than by simple verbal communications. The financial response of the viewers will *far* exceed that of those who only heard the same appeal on the radio, which serves to remind us that, "A picture is, indeed, worth a thousand words!"

Jesus used visual concepts in all His teachings; He taught in parables or "word picture stories" which illustrated divine truth. "All these things Jesus spoke to the multitudes in parables, *and He was not talking to them without a parable.*" (Matt. 13:34; emphasis mine.)

Jesus must have considered this mode of reaching the inner man of His listeners as the most potent and the one most apt to elicit a response, since the Bible is clear that it was the *only* method He used. Jesus knew His audiences would grasp faith more easily if they could *picture* in their minds the truths He was attempting to portray. Centuries have passed, but are we basically any different than they? Certainly not! We are different only in the sense that we have become so intellect oriented that we are not as open to the Holy Spirit and have forsaken the path of simple faith.

I believe that *visualization is basic to faith at any level* and, though it was Jesus' constant mode of conveying truth, it did not begin with Him. Actually, it originated with His Father many centuries earlier.

The fact that God speaks to us in pictures is reflected in the earliest Scriptures, *since visions and dreams have always been the primary language of the Holy Spirit.* Abram (later known as Abraham) and his wife Sarah were childless, and both were advanced in age, being well beyond the normal child-bearing years. Genesis 15:1-6 records a discourse between God and Abram taking place, and it began with: "...and the word of the Lord came to Abram *in a vision...*" (Emphasis mine.)

In verse four God promised Abram that he would yet produce an heir even though it was a physical impossibility. Then God took him outside his tent and said:

> "Now look towards the heavens, and count the stars, if you are able to count them." And He said to him, "So shall your descendants be." (Emphasis mine.)

What was taking place between God and Abram on that ancient, starry night? God was giving Abram an object lesson in parable form, leaving him with a visual focal point (the myriad stars of heaven) for his faith. Since God only spoke verbally to Abram approximately once every fifteen years, it was necessary for him to be able to fix his faith on a reminder of God's promise, something that would be ever before him—so God directed his attention toward the stars.

Verse six says, "...and *then* he believed in the Lord...." When? After God gave him a lesson in visualization; something he could picture as he patiently waited nearly thirty years for the promise to be fulfilled.

Another story similar to this one is found in Genesis 30:25-43 (Please read.) To believe that the rods which Jacob set before the flocks had any *intrinsic* power within themselves to influence the supernatural results which followed would be tantamount to having faith in magic or old wives' tales. They had absolutely *nothing* to do with the subsequent birth of striped/spotted animals. That was a direct outgrowth of *Jacob's* faith. The rods simply served as an adjunct to his faith, *helping him picture or visualize the desired result*—and it worked!

22

FAITH—THAT ELUSIVE COMMODITY

The writer of the Book of Hebrews wrote:

> And without faith it is *impossible* to please Him, for he who comes to God must believe that He is, and that He is a rewarder of those who seek Him. (Heb. 11:6; emphasis mine.)

This verse establishes the highest priority on the procurement of faith for all believers, since there is no other way to please God.

Faith is the single most important topic in Scripture, and presents us with the "which came first, the chicken or the egg?" conundrum, which has puzzled thinkers for years. Faith has always been and ever will be, the precursor of any and *all* the blessings of God. One cannot even receive salvation without it! Likewise, when you received healing (aside from a sovereign act of God), which came first, your healing or faith? (Jesus often said to the person who had just been healed, "Your faith has healed you....") When you received the baptism in the Holy Spirit, which came first? When you received a gift of the Holy Spirit, which came first? Ask a hundred more such questions, and the answer will always be the same—FAITH!

When Jesus said to His disciples in Mark 11:22, "...have faith in God" (literally, in the Greek, "have the faith *of* God"), He was not giving them a friendly suggestion but a direct command. When the translators of the King James Version attempted to interpret this verse they were absolutely stymied by its concept. The thought of *anyone* having the same kind of faith that *God* has was beyond their comprehension and their *doctrinal belief-structure*; so they did the truth a disservice by translating it "have faith *in* God." God expects us to move in the same dimension of faith and power as He did in the Person of Jesus Christ, who had the faith *of* God." Only when we move away from the realm of rational, intellectual reasoning, and into the dimension of (S)spirit, are we enabled to develop and cultivate the dynamics of the faith *of* God in our lives and ministries. The world is groaning to see Christians who will dare to believe that such a life of faith and power is indeed not only possible for this day, but who will produce signs, wonders and miracles as the Holy Spirit's affidavit that the kingdom of God has arrived in their midst!

In every book I have ever read concerning faith, the authors have all been unanimous on one point—faith is always a direct gift from God, and there is nothing anyone can do to produce it. On this point they are quite emphatic. Years ago I would have been in total harmony with that concept, as some of my old sermon tapes will testify, but today I strongly disagree with that view.

Matthew's Gospel records four separate instances in which Jesus chided either His disciples or someone in need, by saying, "O ye of *little faith* (Matt. 6:30; 8:26; 14:31; 16:8; emphasis mine.). The word for "little faith" is *oligopistos* or "puny belief." In the light of what Jesus said, let us examine this issue from the standpoint of those who state that faith is always a direct bestowment from God. Jesus *commanded* us to have the faith *of* God. If faith can only be received as a gift from God (with nothing that *we* can do to produce it), then He would be unfair to judge or reprove us for our lack of it, since it would have been *He* who refused to grant it to us! You simply could not, in good conscience, blame a person for not having something if you were his only source of supply, and you withheld it from him! *If God alone controls the bestowal of faith, or the size of our portion, how could He justify castigating us for our lack of faith?* May I remind you that God is not an "unjust judge." Therefore, it is safe to conclude that *we* have some active role to play in the production and exercise of faith.

Mark 11:20-26 is a brief, yet powerful treatise on faith and there is far more to this passage of Scripture than meets the eye. In verse twenty-three Jesus said:

> Truly, I say to you, whoever *says* to this mountain, "Be taken up and cast into the sea," *and does not doubt in his heart, but believes that what he says is going to happen*, it shall be granted him. (Emphasis mine.)

There is an absolute wealth of Scriptural insight into the "mechanics" of faith presented here but, because of the limitations of our English Bible translations, we miss the subtleties of the Greek language in which it was originally written. In this passage there are three major facts concerning the faith *of* God: 1. We must believe; 2. We must not doubt; 3. The believing and the not doubting take place *in the heart*. At this point some readers may be thinking, "So what's new? What has he just written that isn't obvious?" To answer this legitimate question: nothing—unless we unravel the deeper meanings in the Greek, which were laid aside during translation. Then we will see what Jesus said in a whole new light.

The word "believe" is the verb *pisteuo*, "to believe, also to be persuaded of and hence, to place confidence in, to trust; signifies, in this sense of the word, reliance upon, not only credence.'' This verb comes from the noun *pistis*, ''its chief significance is a conviction respecting God and His Word; persuasion, credence, (belief), moral conviction.''

So, we have here a word which strongly signifies ''believing, persuasion, and conviction respecting God and His Word,'' and carries with it every earmark of *mental activity* (more about that shortly).

The word translated ''doubt'' is the verb *diakrino* which means ''to separate thoroughly, to withdraw from or by implication, to oppose; figuratively, to discriminate; by implication, *decide* or hesitate, waver.'' (The same word is used in James 1:6 where it is translated ''wavering,'' which means ''to be undecided.'') From the word *diakrino* we derive the noun, *diakrisis* which means ''judicial estimation discern, disputation.'' At the root of these words is the word *krino* ''to distinguish, i.e. *to decide mentally* or *judicially* determine.'' This word is used in Acts 21:25, ''we wrote, having decided....'' In examining the phrase ''to decide judicially,'' we find the dictionary definition of ''judicial'' is, ''Suitable for a judge: a judicial mind *considers both sides* of a question.'' There can be absolutely no doubt that all of the aforementioned Greek words deal specifically with a mental action having to do with decision making! (So much for the old adage, ''blind faith.'')

These words indicate that, before faith is ever produced, the believer looks at both sides of the issue and recognizes completely what is at stake for sickness or health, success or failure, winning or losing, etc. When the above review of the circumstances is carried out by a ''renewed mind,'' the final decision regarding a course of action will be based solely upon the Word of God and a revelation of the Father's will for that particular situation.

A perfect example of this is Peter's sojourn on the storm-tossed waters of Galilee where, at the word of the Lord he stepped out of the boat, then ''...*seeing the wind*, he became afraid, and beginning to sink, he cried out....'' (Matt. 14:30; emphasis mine.) His unrenewed mind examined the external manifestations (storm, wind, waves, etc.) surrounding him, ''believed'' the physical evidence, ''doubted'' the supernatural, *and began to sink*. So often doubt is simply ''believing the negative report'' of the physical realm or the senses.

Now we know that to ''not doubt'' means to make a firm decision to accept God at His Word, without wavering (being undecided), and then to stand firm in that belief. Peter trusted Christ, but the circumstances produced doubt and he decided (the Bible says it was due to *fear*) to believe the physical evidence which surrounded him.

The most emphatic truth to be seen here is that *faith is a decision.* When one decides to take a stand on the Word of God, he looks carefully at all the evidence before him, pro and con; examines all the pitfalls, dangers and perils; holds them up alongside the overpowering "evidence of things not seen" (Heb. 11:1b), and makes a conscious decision to believe God!

Now let us examine the phrase, "in his heart." Since this is the arena in which the believing and not doubting take place, it is of primary importance to understand what "heart" means in Scripture. The word is *kardia* from which we derive the word "cardiac," meaning "having to do with the heart." It is absolutely certain that the physical, fleshly pump which we call a heart is *not* what is meant here. The physical heart, which circulates the blood, is the chief organ of physical life ("For the life of the flesh is in the blood...." (Lev. 17:11) and occupies the most important place in the human body. By an easy transition, the word came to stand for man's entire mental and moral activity, both the rational and emotional elements. In other words, the heart is used *figuratively* for the hidden springs of man's personal life.

The Bible describes sin as being "in the heart," because sin is a principle which has its origin in the center of man's inward life, and from there defiles the whole circuit of his actions (Matt. 15:19,20). On the other hand, Scripture regards the heart also as the sphere of Divine influence (Rom. 2:15; Acts 15:19). The heart, lying deep within, contains "the hidden man" (I Pet. 3:4), the real man.

Its usage in the New Testament denotes:

> The seat of physical life (Acts 14:17; Jas. 5:5); the seat of moral nature and *spiritual life*—the seat of grief (Jn. 14:1; Rom. 9:2; II Cor. 2:4); joy (Jn. 16:22; Eph. 5:19); the *desires* (Matt. 5:28; II Pet. 2:14); the affections (Luke 24:32; Acts 21:13); the *perceptions* (Jn. 12:40; Eph. 4:18) the *thoughts* (Matt. 9:4; Heb. 4:12) the understanding (Matt. 13:15; Rom. 1:21); the *reasoning powers* (Mk. 2:6; Luke 24:38); the *imagination* (Luke 1:51); conscience (Acts 2:37; I Jn. 3:20); the *intentions* (Heb. 4:12; I Pet. 4:1); *purpose* (Acts 11:23; II Cor. 9:7); the *will* (Rom. 6:17; Col. 3:15); *FAITH* (Mk. 11:23; Rom. 10:10; Heb. 3:12).

> That if you...believe in your heart that God raised Him from the dead, you shall be saved; for with the *heart* man believes. (Rom. 10:9b,10a; emphasis mine.)

Take care, brethren, lest there should be in any one of you an evil, *unbelieving heart*, in falling away from the living God. (Heb. 3:12; emphasis mine.)

There can be no doubt remaining that when the Bible uses the term *heart* it is a direct reference to the MIND of man. It is obvious that the "heart" referred to in Scripture is the mind, *where the decision-making process takes place*; and this is where either faith or doubt are materialized!

Before you buy a rope with which to hang this "heretic," allow me to define exactly what I believe concerning the mind of man and its ability to "produce" faith. Although it is possible to program the mind to believe something through repeated affirmations (until faith is produced); I am also convinced that this faculty is often misused and abused by Christians and non-Christians alike. Faith should *only* be utilized by Christians to whom it belongs by virtue of divine birthright, and it should *never* be misused to produce *anything* outside the will of God.

This now raises the question, "How can I know the will of God in every circumstance?" Our first and foremost guide is Scripture, whose moral principles and guidelines for "right and wrong" behavior are always correct and which gives a great deal of direction to us. But there are many areas where the Word of God is silent concerning direction in current affairs in our everyday lives. (For instance, how to choose between two equally "right" and worthwhile courses of action?) Thus, the need for meditation: first for ascertaining the will of God; and secondly, for renewing the mind to accept that will. Once we have used the Word and/or meditation (passive, listening meditation) to determine the will of God, we must then engage in active, dynamic meditation to renew or restructure our thought processes until they align themselves with the known will of God. Faith then becomes the supernatural outgrowth of this process!

When Romans 12:2 speaks of the "renewing of the mind," the word for "mind" is *nous* which translates, "the intellect, i.e. mind, understanding." What is, after all, the greatest barrier to faith and the largest supporter of doubt, if not the logical, rational, reasoning mind, which for the most part has been programmed by the world (rather than the Word) and our own five natural senses?

In the Garden of Eden there were two all-important trees—one of life and the other of knowledge. A choice was made and man chose knowledge as opposed to life. His choice has remained basically the same ever since, and his intellect has ruled supreme. The foremost goal which we hope to accomplish through *Christian Meditation* is to teach Christians how to bring every thought captive to the will of God, and to thus begin moving in the same dimension of power and authority as Jesus did. He exercised such a powerfully anointed ministry because He could say that He did nothing except it was something He *saw* the Father doing; that He spoke only those words which He *heard* the Father speaking. His mind was in perfect harmony with the will of the Father, so there was nothing to inhibit the flow of God's unction to minister in the realm of the supernatural.

The Scriptures teach that we can emulate (equal) Jesus' ministry, as He, Himself testified:

> Truly, truly, I say to you, he who believes in Me, the works that I do shall he do also; *and greater works than these shall he do*; because I go to the Father. (Jn. 14:12; emphasis mine.)

This becomes possible only when our minds are yielded to the absolute dominion of the Holy Spirit, to the point where we can say along with the Apostle Paul:

> I have been crucified with Christ; and it is no longer I who live, *but Christ lives in me;* and the life which I now live in the flesh I live by faith in the Son of God, who loved me, and delivered Himself up for me. (Gal. 2:20; emphasis mine.)

If the mind has been programmed to doubt by the input of the world and the natural senses (and it has), why should it not be *de*programmed to allow faith to operate freely? The daily influx of negative thoughts into our minds has been the principal cause of our dearth of faith. It follows then, that it is our responsibility to feed *positive,* Bible-oriented, *faith-producing* thoughts into this mind which, for all of its existence has been plagued by *negative, faith-destroying* thought processes. Not only is there nothing wrong with the practice, but the Bible clearly instructs us to do so!

> Finally, brethren, whatever is true, whatever is honorable, whatever is right, whatever is pure, whatever is lovely, whatever is of good repute, if there is any excellence and anything worthy of praise, *let your mind dwell on these things.* (Phil. 4:8; emphasis mine.)

One of the attributes ascribed to heart was "feelings." Each of us can relate to that meaning, since we all experience some type of emotion many times each day. This should be of prime interest to most of us, since feelings precipitate many of our actions (or inaction), whether good or bad. Feelings (emotions) are most often generated by thoughts (even sub-conscious ones), so it becomes very important to gain control of the mind, and thereby the thought processes which produce emotions. The fact is, that negative thoughts produce negative emotions which contribute to negative actions; they in turn dictate further negative thoughts, actions and results. Many Christians have despaired of ever mastering this seemingly never-ending cycle and their churches have offered no hope or instruction in how to get off this Satanic treadmill. Emotions bark their commands and a host of fine Christians bow in humble obedience, offering the fatalistic excuse, "That's just my nature; it's the way I am; I can't change." Satan loves to hear those words because they are words of defeat. Those days of cowardly surrender are over—for now there is hope! Never again will Christians have to cower before Satan or his emissaries or be led by their emotions into failure and defeat. We have found that we can all learn to bring the "inner man of the heart" (mind) into submission to the (S)spirit within us. The best Scriptural approach to that end is *Christian Meditation*.

Lastly, it is not enough to simply have faith—our words must reflect what our hearts have believed. Paul said in Romans 10:8:

> But what does it say? "The word is near you, in your mouth and in your heart"—that is, the word of faith which we are preaching.

There is a "word of faith" (*rhema*) which is received in our "hearts" (minds) and is then released by the spoken word. As the Bible says:

> The good man out of the good treasure of his heart brings forth what is good; and the evil man out of the evil treasure brings forth what is evil; for his *mouth* speaks from that which fills his *heart (mind, ed.)*. (Luke 6:45; emphasis mine.)

The Bible records at least 64 references in which it makes a definite connection between what is in man's *heart* and what is said with his *mouth*, even linking verbal confession with our salvation:

> That if you confess with your *mouth* Jesus as Lord, and believe in your *heart* that God raised Him from the dead, you shall be sav-

ed; for *with the heart man believes*, resulting in righteousness, and *with the mouth he confesses,* resulting in salvation. (Rom. 10:9,10; emphasis mine.)

Mark 11:23 records the words of Jesus, "...whosoever *believes* that what he *says* is going to happen, it shall be granted him." (Emphasis mine.) The word for "says" means, "to lay forth; relate in words (usually of systematic or set discourse)." *Faith knows exactly what it is appropriating.* Accordingly, you must know very specifically what you desire, and you must clearly and concisely define it! How can one exercise faith for something which is nebulous in his own mind? Often, before healing someone, Jesus would ask, "What do you want me to do for you?" In order to effectively relate your desire and believe for its fulfillment, you must be able to envision (see) what it is you are seeking after.

Once we have determined the will of God, have dealt with (and gotten the mastery over) doubt and cultivated faith through the renewing of our minds by envisioning the promise of God; we will then be able to exercise a boldness of faith-filled speech. We can then expect to experience a whole new life style of faith and expectancy—and a Holy Spirit ministry of power, signs and wonders!

23

EPILOGUE

In researching and writing this book, I have sought only one goal: to open the realm of the (S)spirit to the church, by proving scripturally that Jesus and many other (even Old Testament) people of the Bible regarded a life lived "in the (S)spirit" as the *normal* state of being for God's children. In view of that which we have learned—what is the Christian's responsibility in this area? Is a life of sensitivity and obedience to God's inner voice a matter of choice? (Obviously, to some extent that is true, since all of life is composed of "choices" and many Christians have chosen to live in the "shallows" of Christian experience.) God has not dictated that our complete obedience to Him be an "elective," but a Divine requirement!

We have already seen that many Christians, through ignorance, do not spend time "listening" for God's voice—they simply have no concept that God wants to and *does* speak directly to His children today. After reading this book, you are no longer afforded the "luxury" of such lack of knowledge. You now know it is not only possible to personally hear from God but that it is your responsibility to listen for His voice during your prayertimes and throughout your daily life.

We have also learned that there are many scripturally-sound ways in which we can become sensitive to His voice—through study of the Word and other godly books; through prayer and fasting; through godly conversation and anointed music; and by quieting the mind and flesh through *Christian Meditation*. The ideal is, of course, to utilize all of these, though I have placed the major emphasis of this book on *Christian Meditation* because it has been so sadly neglected by most Christians and misused by many non-Christians for so long.

What is imperative, however, is that by whatever (legitimate) means and by *all* means Christians must hunger for and seek after an intimate relationship with their Creator and Lord! The Twentieth Century Church of Jesus Christ is at the crossroads of destiny: will we become the "glorious" Church spoken of in the Song of Solomon and the Book of Revelation? Will we yield to the flesh and our carnal intellect, or dedicate ourselves to listening for and hearing God's voice?

Having died to give us so much more, Jesus awaits our life-changing decision and still says to us today..."He who has an (spiritual) ear, *let him hear* what the Spirit says...." (Rev. 2:7a; emphasis mine.) **To which our only legitimate reply, born of the (S)spirit, will be: "...***Speak, Lord, for thy servant is listening.***"** (I Sam. 3:9b; emphasis mine.)

Catalog of books and tapes available by writing:

Rev. Burton W. Seavey
1100 N. East Avenue
Oak Park, IL 60302

Quantity discounts on this book available upon request.

Pastors and Christian leaders interested in hosting a CHRISTIAN MEDITATION SEMINAR should contact the author at the above address for particulars.